Identifying the Righteous Marjiʿiyyah

I0517294

Āyatullāh Sayyid
Munīr al-Khabbāz

AL-BURĀQ
Heighten The Mind

Copyright

ISBN: 978-1-956276-18-3
Printed and published by al-Burāq Publications.
Translated and annotated by al-Burāq Publications. Where needed, context and transliterations were added. Some minor edits were made to the translated Arabic text.

www.al-Buraq.org
publications@al-Buraq.org
First Edition | April 2022

Dedication

The publication of this book was made possible through the generous support of our donors.

بسم الله الرحمن الرحيم
الحمد لله رب العالمين الرحمن الرحيم
مالك يوم الدين إياك نعبد وإياك نستعين
اهدنا الصراط المستقيم صراط الذين
أنعمت عليهم غير المغضوب عليهم
ولا الضالين

Please recite *Sūrah al-Fātiha* and ask Allāh for the Divine reward (*thawāb*) to be conferred upon the donors and also the souls of all the deceased in whose memory their loved ones have contributed graciously towards the publication of *Identifying the Righteous Marji'iyyah.*

We begin by giving all praise and thanks to God ﷿ for giving us the tawfiq to translate this book. He has guided us and without Him, we would not have been guided to the straight path embodied by the Prophet Muḥammad ﷺ and the Ahl al-Bayt عليهم السلام.

This book is dedicated to Āyatullāh Sayyid Munīr al-Khabbāz and all the scholars, martyrs and believers who worked tirelessly to promote the pure Muḥammadan path.

We want to also give our thanks and appreciation to all believers from around the world and acknowledge the team which helped al-Burāq Publications complete this work, spending countless hours to make its publication possible. Please recite Sūrah al-Fātiḥah on behalf of them and their marḥūmīn.

This book is dedicated in honor of the following individuals. Please remember them in your prayers and may God ﷿ have mercy on them and their loved ones.

Abdullah Anwar

Afifeh Awad

Ahmad Watfa

Aisha El-Mekki

Akram Badaoui

Sayed Sobh Hamid Sobh

Alam Ara

Ali Ftouni

Ali Aoun

Ali Tufekcic

Alya Agemy

Amina Begum

Band-e-khuda

Basima Awad

Brett Johnson

Farhat Naqvi

Fida Hussain

Habeeb Mohessin

Hajj Haidar Alaouie

Hajj Ahmad Chit

Hajj Ali Hammoud

Hajj Deeb Aoun

Hajj Hassan Sobh

Hajj Mohsen Amen

Hajj Sami Ftouni

Hajji Amneh Sobh-Ftouni

Hajji Hiam Hojeije

Hajji Iman Elsaghir

Hajji Raida Bazzi

Hajji Sobhia Aoun

Humayun Ali Baig

Hussain Shaheedi

Hussein Saab

Sayyid Khomeini قدس سره

Jayh Seng

Julie Ann Troupe

Latifa T. Barnett

Mahmoud Tiba

Majida Hassan

Majida Musavi

Makarem Awad

Malika Begum

Maryam Abdullah
Mashadi Musavi
Masooma Begun
Mirza Mazher Baig
Mohammad Atia
Munawwar Jehan
Musharaf Fatima
Nisrine Fahs
Noor Aoun
Razia Sarfaraz
Sagheera Khatoon
Sardar
Sayed Hussain Alqallaf
Shaker Khayat
Shandar Fatima
Syed Abbas Kazmi
Syed Ahsan Rizvi
Syed Fidvi Ali
Syed Hasan Jafri
Syed Irtiza Rizvi
Syed Mehdi Ahmed
Syed Mehdi Rizvi
Syed Mujtaba Ahmed
Syed Mujtaba Rizvi
Syed Muntazir Naqvi
Syed Nawab Kazmi
Syed Nurul Jafri
Syed Oqail Ahmed
Syed Tehmaaz Kazmi
Syed Tilmiz Rizvi
Syed Yousuf Hussain
Syeda Batool
Syeda Birjis Fatima
Syeda Saeeda Begum
Talal Al Haj Hussein
Tamara Oldenburg
Taqia Naqvi
Turfah Sobh
Youssef Dabaja
Youssef Abadi
Zaheer Agha
Zahra Hisse
Zakiya Begum

Duaa al-Hujja

اللهم كن لوليك الحجة بن الحسن صلواتك
عليه وعلى آبائه في هذه الساعة وفي كل
ساعة وليا وحافظا وقائدا وناصرا ودليلا
وعينا حتى تسكنه أرضك طوعا وتمتعه فيها طويلا

O Allah, be, for Your representative, the Hujjat (proof), son of al-Hasan, Your blessings be upon him and his forefathers, in this hour and in every hour: a guardian, a protector, a leader, a helper, a proof, and an eye - until You make him live on the Earth, in obedience (to You), and cause him to live in it for a long time.

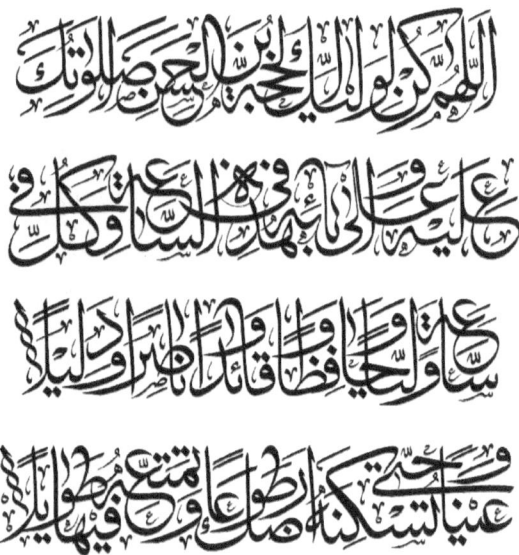

Terms of Respect

The following Arabic phrases have been used throughout this book in their respective places to show the reverence which the noble personalities deserve.

عزّ وجلّ

Used for God, meaning:
Exalted and Sublime (Perfect) is He

صلى الله عليه وآله

Used for Prophet Muḥammad, meaning:
Blessings from God be upon him and his family

عليه السلام

Used for a man (singular) of a high status, meaning:
Peace be upon him

عليها السلام

Used for a woman (singular) of a high status, meaning:
Peace be upon her

عليهما السلام

Used for men/women (dual) of a high status, meaning:
Peace be upon them both

عليهم السلام

Used for men and/or women (plural) of a high status, meaning:
Peace be upon them all

قدس سره

Used for a deceased scholar, meaning:
May his resting [burial] place remain pure

عجل الله تعالى فرجه الشريف

Used for Imām Muḥammad al-Mahdī, meaning:
May God hasten his return

Transliteration Table

The method of transliteration of Islamic terminology from the Arabic language has been carried out according to the standard transliteration table below.

ء	ʾ	ر	r	ف	f
ا	a	ز	z	ق	q
ب	b	س	s	ك	k
ت	t	ش	sh	ل	l
ث	th	ص	ṣ	م	m
ج	j	ض	ḍ	ن	n
ح	ḥ	ط	ṭ	و	w
خ	kh	ظ	ẓ	ه	h
د	d	ع	ʿ	ي	y
ذ	dh	غ	gh		
Long Vowels					
ا	ā	و	ū	ي	ī
Short Vowels					
ـَـ	a	ـُـ	u	ـِـ	i

Table of Contents

About the Author

Sayyid Munīr al-Khabbāz was born in Qatif, Saudi Arabia in 1384 AH (1964 CE). At the age of 14, Sayyid Munīr traveled to the Holy City of Najaf to begin his training within the Islamic seminary. Not long after, he migrated towards the city of Qum, Iran, when the Baathist Regime in Iraq began tightening its crackdown on the Islamic seminary.

In the year 1402 AH (1981 CE), Sayyid Munīr returned to Qatif for personal reasons and continued his studies there. One year later, he traveled to Damascus, Syria to study in the Islamic seminary there under the tutelage of His Eminence Sayyid Jamāl al-Khū'ī. Finally, in 1405 AH (1984 CE), he returned to the Holy City of Najaf to continue his studies. There, he studied under some of the most respected scholars of the Islamic seminary, including Grand Āyatullāh Sayyid Abū l-Qāsim al-Mūsawī al-Khū'ī and Grand Āyatullāh Murtaḍā al-Burūjirdī. With the recommendation of another one of his tutors, Sayyid Ḥabib Ḥusaynian, Sayyid Munīr also began to study under the tutelage of Grand Āyatullāh Sayyid 'Alī al-Sistānī, benefitting much from his lessons in the principles of jurisprudence, as well as his extensive examination of modern sciences and their correlation with Islamic sciences.

Sayyid Munīr then moved back to Qum where he studied under Grand Āyatullāh Waḥīd Khurāsānī for several years. He also studied extensively under the tutelage of Grand Āyatullāh Mīrzā Jawād al-Tabrīzī, who became a guide and mentor for the remainder of his life. Before his passing, Grand Āyatullāh al-Tabrīzī gave Sayyid Munīr an endorsement as a jurist capable of deducing Islamic laws from its sources.

In 1418 AH (1997 CE), Sayyid Munīr began teaching Advanced Seminars (Bahth Kharij) in jurisprudence. He is known by his students for his eloquence, as well as his encouragement of discussion and debate. He is an avid lecturer and an author, with multiple works published for a varied readership.

Preface

بسم الله الرحمن الرحيم

In the Name of God, the Beneficent,
the Merciful

All praise belongs to God, Lord of all the worlds, and may God send His blessings on Muḥammad and his pure family.

Despite the long absence of the Imām of the Age عجل الله تعالى فرجه الشريف and the events and hardships that have struck the *umma*, God عزّ وجلّ has granted this *umma* men who will preserve it from being lost, strengthen it and lead it to goodness and righteousness.

This path was upheld since the greater occultation (*al-ghayba al-kubrā*) until today, by a group of chosen figures. Of those figures is the great *marja'* of the rightful sect, the Grand Āyatullāh Sayyid 'Alī al-Sistānī, may God عزّ وجلّ preserve him. Sayyid al-Sistānī remained in Najaf for a long time, away from the spotlight and the media until Divine Will decided to present him to the world. From then on, he stated his noble positions that were a safety valve for the *umma*, preserving it from division and ceasing bloodshed; although the extremists wanted it to continue.

These glowing pages reveal some aspects of this great figure through a lecture given by Āyatullāh Sayyid

Munīr al-Khabbāz in the holy city of Qum in 1428 A.H. Who is more worthy of such a deed than Sayyid Munīr, who was Sayyid al-Sistānī's student, benefitting from his vast knowledge and living closely by his side?

May God send His blessings on Muḥammad and his pure family ﷺ.

Overview of the Marjiʿiyyah

بسم الله الرحمن الرحيم

In the Name of God, the Beneficent,
the Merciful

In the name of God, and peace and blessings be upon al-Muṣṭafā and his pure family.

This introduction involves several points. The first point is the strength of the Imāmī sect, which lies in the rallying of the Imāmī Shīʿīs around the position of the *Marjiʿiyyah*. Aside from the *Marjiʿiyyah*, there is no popular, authoritative Islamic leadership whom millions of Muslims obey. The word of the *Marjiʿiyyah* assumes pride of place when it comes to effective commanding and forbidding.

The second point is the power of the *Marjiʿiyyah*. The secret behind the power of the *Marjiʿiyyah* goes back to its sanctified status among people. For the Imāmīs, the *Marjiʿiyyah* is an extension of the position of the infallible (*maʿṣūm*) Imām عليه السلام. The *Marjiʿiyyah* acquired its sanctity from two factors: encompassing the knowledge of Ahl al-Bayt عليهم السلام and piety (*taqwa*). If the position of *Marjiʿiyyah* was a government position, or a position subject to popular election, or a position based on military power, financial fortune, or media mouthpieces, it wouldn't have acquired this unique sanctity that causes millions of Shīʿīs to sacrifice their lives, children, and money at a word issued by the *Marjiʿiyyah*.

For this reason, the enemies of religion and the Shīʿī sect strove to criticize the *Marjiʿiyyah* and doubt its sanctity and integrity over the past few years. The purpose of this is to belittle the *Marjiʿiyyah* in the eyes of the people and eliminate the Imāmī sect's power.

The third point is that the position of *Marjiʿiyyah* involves three duties:

1. Issuing legal decrees (*iftāʾ*): Issuing legal decrees means that the jurist's legal decrees are valid for other people. If a commoner (*ʿammī*) acts according to a jurist's legal decree, this decree will be the commoner's excuse before God.

2. Judging: The *marjaʿ* has the final word in disputes and conflicts, his ruling is final and irrefutable, and it has to be obeyed. It is even prohibited for another jurist to contradict his ruling, unless it was proven that the *marjaʿ* had based himself on the testimony of people who are not upright (*khaṭaʾ al-istinād*) or

people who are upright but mixed up (*khaṭa' al-mustanad*).[1]

3. Guardianship: Jurists differed about the limits of the guardianship of the jurist, forming two different groups. The first group believes in guardianship in relation to matters of social order (*al-umūr al-ḥisbiyya*). The definition of *al-umūr al-ḥisbiyya* is that they are matters that are the basis of preserving order, including the preservation of life, dignity, and monetary sources. For this reason, it is definitively concluded that the Lawgiver would not be pleased if such matters were neglected. An example is preserving public and private monetary sources, such as the money of orphans and religious endowments (*awqāf*).

The proof in support of the guardian of the jurist is that preserving monetary sources, for example, depends on managing them, which requires guardianship; in the

---

[1] [Translator's note]: Elsewhere, Sayyid Munīr gives the following example to clarify the meaning of the terms *khaṭa' al-istinād* and *khaṭa' al-mustanad*. If two witnesses tell a jurist that dealing with a certain company involves committing prohibited deeds, but it was later revealed that these witnesses were not upright individuals, this is classified as *khaṭa' istinād*. If, on the other hand, the witnesses were upright individuals but mixed up the names of one company with another, this is classified as *khaṭa' al-mustanad*. See https://almoneer.org/?act=artc&id=722

very least, it is certain that the upright jurist has guardianship.

The second group believes in absolute guardianship across all matters and domains, which is general guardianship. General guardianship means that whenever public interest (*al-maṣlaḥa al-'āmma*) requires the jurist to issue a command, pronounce a prohibition, or act in a certain way, he may do so. The jurist's ruling is valid even when the intended interest is supplementary (*kamāliyya*) and unnecessary for the preservation of order. Examples of supplementary interests are enforcing laws to improve education, increase production, and pave roads, among other supplementary interests.

Absolute guardianship was discussed by al-Narrāqī ﵀, *al-'Awā'id*, 550; Muḥammad Ḥasan al-Najafī ﵀, *al-Jawāhir*, 21/396; Shaykh al-Anṣārī ﵀, *al-Makāsib*, 3/554; Imām Khomeini ﵀ , *Kitāb al-Bay'*, 2/617. In this book, Imām Khomeini ﵀ said, "An upright jurist is entitled to everything that is the Prophet's and the Imāms' in relation to governing and politics" and "Based on interests, the jurists give the people commands that may be issued by the governor (*wālī*), and they must be obeyed."

If we go back to the books that refer to this topic, we find that there are many issues under discussion. The first issue is this. Is the jurist entitled to lead an armed uprising against the rulers of his time and establish an Islamic government even if this leads to the loss of life and money? There are many narrations in section 13 of the chapter on waging *jihād* against enemies in volume 15 of *Wasā'il al-Shī'a*, and the jurists differed about them. Do these narrations mean that armed uprising is absolutely prohibited or do they mean that armed uprising is prohibited only if the upriser is calling the people to obey him? Do these narrations point to a secondary issue which is that those who rise up to establish a state will not be successful but will face tribulations that will subject the Shī'a to further hardship? Were these narrations issued in a state of dissimulation (*taqiyya*), and so they are not to be taken in consideration?

Some jurists believe these narrations are in opposition to the Qur'ān, and so they are refused for contradicting the Book, such as God's saying, "Indeed God enjoins justice and kindness"[2] and "and, when you judge between people, to judge with fairness."[3] An alternative to refusing these narrations is relating them to the time of Imām al-Ṣādiq 📿 and the aftermath of Zayd ibn 'Alī's movement. This is discussed in detail in the relevant sources, and it is left to those most knowledgeable about it, i.e. to the masters of jurisprudence.

---

[2] Sūrat al-Naḥl, verse 90.

[3] Sūrat al-Nisā', verse 58.

The second issue is that it is certain that the infallible Imām ﷺ has mandated guardianship (*wilāya taklīfiyya*) as well as declaratory guardianship (*wilāya waḍʿiyya*). Obligation-based guardianship involves obeying the Imām's ﷺ commands and prohibitions in relation to political and administrative issues. Positivistic guardianship is his authority over the affairs of governing and public funds, as well as over people and money. This is based on the verse: "The Prophet has a greater authority over the faithful than they have over their own selves."[4] If public interest required the Imām ﷺ to command people to pay a certain tax, he ﷺ should be obeyed. Similarly, if public interest required him ﷺ to interfere with people's property for the sake of constructing a public road or a bridge, his ﷺ actions are to be obeyed. Does guardianship, in its obligation-based and positivistic branches, apply to the jurist as well?

The third issue concerns the proof in support of the general guardianship of the jurist. If we go back to the chapter on selling (*al-bayʿ*) in the books of jurisprudence, we find that the proofs given to support general guardianship are of two types: rational (*ʿaqlī*) and transmitted (*naqlī*). The transmitted proofs include the narration without a chain of transmission in *Man Lā Yaḥḍuruh al-Faqīh*, 4/520; the narration of al-

---

[4] Sūrat al-Aḥzāb, verse 6.

Baṭā'inī in *al-Wasā'il*, 3/284; the trustworthy narration of al-Sakūnī in *al-Kāfī*, 1/34; the narration of Abī Khadīja in *al-Wasā'il*, 27/139; and the sound narration of al-Qaddāḥ in *al-Kāfī*, 1/34. All these and other narrations have been investigated in regard to their content or chain of transmission, such as the accepted narration of 'Umar ibn Ḥanẓala, and the rescript (*tawqī'*) [of Imām Mahdī] concerning Isḥāq ibn Ya'qūb. Their chains of transmission and the fact that they prove general guardianship have been discussed. Also discussed was the meaning of the verse: "O you who have faith! Obey God and obey the Prophet and those vested with authority among you."[5] It was concluded that the verse referred to the Imāms ﷺ or the jurists more generally.

As for the rational proofs, they may be summarized in two points. The first point is this. Imām Khomeini ﷺ said in *Kitāb al-Bay'*, 2/620, that the proof of Imāmate is the proof of the necessity of governing through the guardianship of the jurist during the age of occultation. This is because it is necessary to spread justice, teaching (*ta'līm*), and education (*tarbiya*), uphold order, and guard the frontiers of Islamic world. On the opposite ends of the spectrum, there are others who believe that the proof of the Imāmate does not include establishing a government and spreading justice. These two things

[5] Sūrat al-Nisā', verse 59.

are obligations of all Muslims if they are able to do them. The proof of Imāmate, for these people, is reason's ruling about the necessity of a Proof who may be referred back to regarding the principles and branches of the Sharīʿa. This is regardless of whether this Proof was able to establish a government, as in the case of Imām ʿAlī عليه السلام, or not, as in the case of the other Imāms عليهم السلام.

In other words, does the necessity of the presence of the Imām عليه السلام as an extension of the Prophet ﷺ prove the general guardianship of whoever is able to spread fairness and justice, apply the rulings of Islamic law, and guard the frontiers of Islamic world? If this is the case, this same necessity dictates the general guardianship of the jurist who possesses all the required conditions during the age of the occultation for the same purpose and goal. Another possibility is the necessity of the existence of the Imām عليه السلام based on the necessity of the existence of a Proof of God to act as a reference who explains the rulings of everything and explains the noble Qur'ān: "so that mankind may not have any argument against God, after the [sending of the] apostles."[6] In this case, the guardianship of the jurist during the age of occultation is not required.

Yes, the case is different for the infallible Imām عليه السلام. Rationally, based on his infallibility, and on the position

[6] Sūrat al-Nisā', verse 165.

of Imāmate – given to him ﷺ by God ﷻ – over all creation, in all their affairs, the Imām ﷺ has guardianship over all the affairs of every person other than himself. If this was not the case, the Imām ﷺ would not be the Imām of every person concerning all matters. Specific texts have indicated this as well.

The second point is this. Do the rulings, punitive laws, and punishments indicate that the jurist has general guardianship that allows him to implement them? If not, the legislation of such laws would be futile. In addition, the call for establishing justice on earth in the Qur'ān and *sunna* requires general guardianship; or else it would be no more than empty words. However, is the purpose of such calls to indicate that they are required of all capable Muslims, and not of jurists specifically, as a collective obligation (*wājib kifā'ī*)?

Imām Khomeini ؒ said that[7] divine rulings related to financial affairs, politics, and rights have not been abrogated; they are valid until the Day of Judgment. The very fact that these rulings persist indicates the necessity of a government and a guardianship that guarantee the sovereignty and application of the divine law.

On page 626, Imām Khomeini ؒ says, "The upright jurist is accorded everything given to the Prophet and

[7] See *Kitāb al-Bayʿ*, 2/619.

the Imāms in the domains of government and politics. It is absurd to differentiate in this regard, because the guardian, whoever he may be, is the one who applies the rulings of the Sharīʿa, enforces the divine punishments, and receives the land tax and other taxes and spends them upon the welfare of the Muslims."

On the other hand, there are some who believe that applying these laws and rulings is necessary, but it is the collective obligation of Islamic society to do so. It is enough if this responsibility is assumed by a trustworthy person or a committee of trustworthy people who are knowledgeable about the rulings of the Sharīʿa. However, this does not prove the general guardianship of the jurist.

Yes, when order depends on enforcing these laws, and when their enforcement depends on the jurist's interference, the jurist has guardianship but not because he is a jurist. His guardianship stems from the fact that maintaining order depends on him, and it is a part of guardianship's role.

It is important to note that the general guardianship of the jurist is a juristic discussion among the experts of jurisprudence. By presenting the different proofs, I only wanted to point them out, not give precedence of one opinion over another.

The fourth issue is this: Are jurists who deny the general guardianship of the jurist also denying the jurist's guardianship in managing order in the land of the Muslims, defending its frontiers, and applying the laws that preserve lives, dignities, and money? Do those who deny the general guardianship of the jurist believe that jurists do not have any active role? The truth is that all jurists believe that a jurist has a central role. In Imāmī jurisprudence, there are no jurists who limit the role of *Marjiʿiyyah* to writing a scholarly treatise. *Marjiʿiyyah* has three functions, but there is a difference about the scope of the third function. This becomes clear upon reviewing the words of the Sayyid of the sect, Imām al-Khūʾī قدس سره,[8] who mentions that the *Marjiʿiyyah* has guardianship over matters of social order that it would displease the Lawgiver to have ignored.

This concept was clarified by the jurist of his age, Shaykh al-Tabrīzī قدس سره, who was Imām al-Khūʾī's قدس سره student. Shaykh al-Tabrīzī قدس سره said, "Matters of social order are all the things about which is known that the Lawgiver requires without assigning a specific person to undertake them. Among them, and the most important of them, is managing order in the country and providing equipment and organizing preparations to defend it."[9]

---

[8] See *Kitāb al-Tanqīḥ*, 1/423-25 and *Mustanad al-ʿUrwa*, 2/88-89.

[9] See *Ṣirāṭ al-Najāt*, 1/10.

In his book, Shaykh al-Tabrīzī ﷺ said, "Matters of social order include the money of the treasury, public endowments (*al-mawqūfāt al-ʿāmma*), punishments (*ḥudūd*) and discretionary punishments (*tazʿīr*), and receiving religious dues (*al-ḥuqūq al-sharʿiyya*) and spending them as needed."[10] Sayyid al-Khū'ī ﷺ went even farther than many jurists in his legal decree (*fatwa*), stating that preemptive *jihād* (*jihād ibtidā'ī*) is obligatory during the age of occultation. Sayyid al-Khū'ī ﷺ said that if the Muslims possessed the equipment, arms, and ability, it is their obligation to wage *jihād* against unbelievers and call them to Islam. Speaking about *jihād* in *Minhāj al-Ṣāliḥīn*, Sayyid al-Khū'ī ﷺ said, "Since undertaking this important matter [*jihād*] abroad requires a leader and a commander who the Muslims should obey, these requirements inevitably apply to the jurist who fulfills all the necessary conditions. The jurist should undertake this important matter in consideration of social order (*min bāb al-ḥisba*), since if anyone else undertakes it, this would result in chaos."[11]

Sayyid al-Khū'ī ﷺ clearly states that the jurist has guardianship over waging *jihād* as it requires sacrificing lives and money, and guardianship over preserving order in Muslim lands, in addition to preventing chaos in

---

10 *Irshād al-Ṭālib*, 3/26.

11 *Minhāj al-Ṣāliḥīn*, 1/366.

Islamic society. This is because the jurist has guardianship over the things that order depends upon. Whoever believes that the jurist has guardianship over *jihād* should more primarily believe in his guardianship over order in the country."[12]

The conclusion is that the jurist has guardianship over all things relating to maintaining order and stability. Sayyid al-Khū'ī ☙ referred to this in his statements during the 1991 uprising (*al-intifāḍa al-Sha'bāniyya*), stating that he assumed leadership of the people at that time based on the necessity of maintaining order,[13] and established a committee of religious scholars to run the country. The bottom line is that there is no difference between the jurists who believe in general guardianship when it comes to matters of social order; both sides believe that the jurist has a leadership role in society if he is able to perform it. The difference simply lies in two questions.

The first question is the following. Is the jurist's guardianship in managing order due to a particularity that the jurist possesses or is it because the jurist is at least certainly among those who have guardianship over

---

[12] Sayyid al-Khū'ī also pointed this out in *al-Mu'tamad fil-Qaḍā' wal-Shahādāt*, 73.

[13] One of Sayyid al-Khū'ī's statements during *al-intifāḍa al-Sha'bāniyya*.

maintaining order? The second question is this. Is the guardianship of the jurist as broad as the guardianship of the infallible ﷺ, extending to supplementary interests, or is the guardianship of the jurist specifically concerned with public interests that are related to maintaining Islamic order? In the second case, people would have guardianship over other aspects and act accordingly.

The fourth issue is the origin of a *marjaʿ's* scholarly value; where does a *marjaʿ's* scholarly value come from? In answer, there are two opinions. The first opinion is called the scholarly characteristic of a Shīʿī *marjaʿ*. This characteristic is based on the concept of becoming learned in religion that was mentioned in the verse: "But why should not there go forth a group from each of their sections to become learned in religion?"[14] This concept encompasses knowledge of the sciences of religion, whether the principles or branches of religion, doctrine, and jurisprudence. This is what God ﷻ means by the word "religion," as religion is not limited to jurisprudence. Religion is the meaning of God's ﷻ saying, "and to warn their people when they return to them, so that they may beware."[15] Warning is a general function.

[14] Sūrat al-Tawba, verse 122.

[15] Sūrat al-Tawba, verse 122.

This is also the point of the sound *ḥadīth* narrated by Ya'qūb ibn Shu'ayb. He said, "I said to Abī 'Abdillāh, 'If something happened to the Imām, what should the people do?' He replied, "Did you forget the verse: '"But why should not there go forth a group from each of their sections to become learned in religion and to warn their people when they return to them, so that they may beware?"[16] Those who go forth are excused as long as they are seeking answers, and those who await them are excused until the seekers return." This narration means that the knowledge of the Imām ﷺ includes becoming learned in religion (*tafaqquh*).

This has two results. The first result is that the criterion of the *mujtahid*'s scholarliness and being most learned (*a'lamiyya*) is his brilliance in the sciences of jurisprudence and theology (*kalam*), i.e. doctrine, and not jurisprudence alone. It is noteworthy that the verse seemingly refers to the seekers warning about things they have become learned in religion about; in other words, it does not seem that the verse implies the comprehensive warning about all that constitutes knowledge. The context of the verse simply states that what's required is warning about things scholars have become learned about. The most important thing is the presence of learnedness in religion, including the knowledge of more than the branches of religion.

[16] Sūrat al-Tawba, verse 122.

However, one might pause at the existence of learning religion (*tafaqquh al-dīn)* and becoming learned *in* religion (*al-tafaqquh fī al-dīn*).

If the scope is the science of doctrine, the science of doctrine is learning religion in itself because doctrine is the pillar of religion and fits the meaning of learning religion. However, if the scope is the knowledge of religious rulings, that constitutes becoming learned in religion.

Even though the narration indicates that the learning in the verse includes the knowledge of the Imām ﷺ, it does not indicate that learning includes the knowledge of doctrines. Imām al-ʿAskarī ﷺ said, "commoners may emulate a jurist who conducts himself decorously (*ṣā'inan li-nafsihi*), observes his religion (*ḥāfiẓan li-dīnihi*), contradicts his desire (*mukhālifan hawāh*) and obeys his Master." Becoming learned in religion in the verse includes the knowledge of the Imām ﷺ based on practical application and not verbal proof. If the verse in itself indicated knowledge of both the principles and branches of religion under the headline of becoming learned in religion, it does not indicate the authoritativeness (*ḥujjiyya*) of the jurist's opinion in the principles and branches of religion. The extent of the meaning of the verse is the authoritativeness of a trustworthy person's (*al-thiqa*) report about what they know, whether it counts among the branches of religion or among doctrinal issues, like the knowledge of the Imām ؑ.

The second result is emulation (*taqlīd*) in doctrinal matters. Is the jurist a reference in jurisprudential matters and doctrinal matters as well? In other words, is the jurist's opinion authoritative for non-jurists at both levels or is a jurist only authoritative in jurisprudential matters? There are two opinions in this regard.

The first opinion is that the jurist's opinion is totally authoritative, and that is for two reasons. The first reason is the presence of narrations that praise the jurists, such as Imām al-Ṣādiq's ؑ saying, "The jurists are the trustees of the messengers." Since the messengers communicate jurisprudence and doctrine from God, their trustees are like them. Imām al-Kāẓim ؑ said, "The jurists are the strongholds of Islam." A jurist cannot be the stronghold of Islam unless he was a reference in jurisprudence and doctrine. Imām al-Ṣādiq ؑ also said, "The scholars are the inheritors of the prophets." This means that the scholars' legacy also includes the knowledge of doctrine. Similar to these narrations are the texts commanding people to draw knowledge from the jurists. An example is Imām al-Riḍā's ؑ response to the person who asked, "Who should I learn the markers (*maʿālim*) of my religion from?" The response was, "From Zakariyyā ibn Ādam al-Qummī, who is reliable (*maʾmūn*) in matters of religion and this world." When Imām al-Riḍā ؑ was asked, "Is Yūnus ibn ʿAbdullāh trustworthy (*thiqa*) for me to take the markers of my religion from him?", he ﷺ said, "Yes." Clearly, the phrase "markers of religion" includes both the principles and branches of religion.

The second reason is the reasonable custom (*al-sīra al-ʿuqalāʾiyya*) of considering the opinion of an expert authoritative in their area of expertise. A consequence of that is the authoritativeness of a jurist's opinion in doctrinal matters that can only be reached by the jurist.

The second opinion is that the jurist's opinion is only authoritative in jurisprudential matters, in contrast to the proofs of the first opinion. The first proof of the second opinion requires careful consideration (*fīhi taʾammul*). It states that the narrations that praise the jurists have weak chains of transmission. In addition, using the first and third narrations as proof generalizes the predicate (*maḥmūl*) to prove the inclusion of the trusteeship and inheritance of prophets in the knowledge of doctrine. This is although the sources state that an informative sentence (*jumla khabariyya*) highlights the relation of the predicate to the subject (*al-mawḍūʿ*); it does not highlight the predicate itself such that the predicate may be generalized.

If someone said, "Zayd is a writer," it does not mean that Zayd is familiar with all kinds of writing, and if someone said, "Zayd is knowledgeable," it does not mean that Zayd is familiar with all branches of knowledge. The same applies to the Imām's 🕮 mention of the trusteeship of the messengers and the inheritance of the prophets. It does not include all the knowledge of the prophets, or else the jurists would have been familiar with the prophets' knowledge of the unseen (*al-ʿulūm al-ghaybiyya*).

As for referring to the jurists as the strongholds of Islam, it is true that it indicates that defending Islam is of the jurist's duties. However, there is no correlation between a jurist's duty and obligation to defend Islam and the authoritativeness of his opinion in doctrinal matters. In addition, the narrations that command learning require pause for two reasons. The first reason is that perhaps the command to learn religion from these elect persons, such as Zakariyyā ibn Ādam and Yūnus ibn ʿAbdullāh and their likes, may be based on the fact that their narrations actually inspire security and trust due to their closeness to the Imām and due to their elevated scholarly level. These narrations do not have to mean that the jurist is authoritative. The second reason is that perhaps the point of these narrations is the authoritativeness of the report that comes from a trustworthy person, whether in jurisprudential or doctrinal matters and not the authoritativeness of the jurist. For this reason, these narrations have no weight when it comes to the authoritativeness of the jurist's opinion.

As for the second proof of the second opinion, it is that doctrines are divided into two parts. The first part includes doctrines that require having knowledge of them because their proofs are definitive, such as the principles of religion and the matters related to them, like infallibility and guardianship. The second part includes doctrines that don't require knowledge; if there are proofs for them, they may simply be believed in.

Obviously, the mere opinion of a scholar doesn't generate certainty. Yes, if knowledge results from the saying of the scholar, it would be a proof and an excuse for the commoner. As for the second part of doctrines, which require proof to be believed in, the validity of emulating scholars regarding them lacks additional proof aside from custom (*sīra*). Custom is thematic proof (*dalīl lubbī*), as it has been said in the science of jurisprudence.[17] Thematic proofs are restricted to their certain aspects; the certain aspects of thematic proofs produce an external action. External actions only result from jurisprudential matters and not doctrinal matters, and particularly not the matters that the religiously accountable person (*al-mukallaf*) is required to believe in in advance. Yes, if the religiously accountable person achieves certainty due to the jurist's words, this certainty itself would be the proof, and not the words of the jurist.

The second opinion on the origin of a *marjaʿ's* value is that it comes from the position of scholarliness. A jurist's scholarliness results from consideration (*naẓar*) and trustworthiness (*amāna*). Consideration is mentioned in the acceptable narration "[he who] narrates our *ḥadīth* and considers our *ḥalāl* and

---

[17] [Translator's note]: For more on the term "thematic proof," consider the following: "[C]onsensus as it is consensus would have no value in Shīʿa jurisprudence should it not reveal opinion of the infallible-innocent personality, and that is why it is not considered a free-standing source for religious precepts... [A]uthority is for the revealed, i.e., [the *sunna*], and not for the revealer, i.e., consensus; and consensus precisely plays the role of massive report – with one difference: the latter [i.e. report] reveals the very words of the infallible-innocent personality and that is why it is called lexical proof (*al-dalīl al-lafẓī*) while the former [consensus] reveals the opinion of the infallible-innocent personality and not his words and that is why it is called thematic proof (*al-dalīl al-lubbī*) which conveys the theme and not the terms." See Alireza Hodaee, *An Introduction to Methodology of Islamic Jurisprudence (Uṣūl al-Fiqh): A Shiite Approach*, 135.

ḥarām." As for trustworthiness, the narration from Imām al-Ḥusayn ﷺ states: "The course of matters and rulings should be conducted by those who know God and who are trustworthy about His *ḥalāl* and *ḥarām*." For this reason, we say the following.

The jurist acquires his scholarly characteristic through study in the seminary. A seminary student should study all the sciences related to understanding the narrations of Ahl al-Bayt ﷺ and proving the rightfulness of the religion and the sect through knowledge of doctrinal sciences using sources such as *Sharḥ al-Bāb al-Ḥādī ʿAshar*, *Sharḥ Tajrīd al-Iʿtiqād*, and others. Afterward, the jurist studies the texts discussing original branches of knowledge (*al-maʿārif al-aṣliyya*) such as *Kitāb al-Kāfī* and other books so that he may be fully knowledgeable.

In his *al-Bayān*, Sayyid al-Khūʾī ﷺ discussed change in divine decision (*al-badāʾ*) based on the texts, as well as disproving the accusation [of the Shīʿa] of believing in the distortion of the Qurʾān by way of omission (*bi-naḥw al-naqīṣa*) based on sound texts. Sayyid al-Khūʾī also discussed the truth of divine will in the lectures of the second part of the principles of jurisprudence, the impurity of the unbeliever, and the centrality of actual Islam (*al-Islām al-wāqiʿī*) and not conceptual Islam (*al-Islām al-iʿtibārī*).

In his *al-Anwār al-Ilāhiyya*, Shaykh al-Tabrīzī ﷺ discussed the necessity of the presence of an Imām in every age as well as the necessity of absolute infallibility based on the texts. In his lesson on the opposition of legal proofs that was written down by his student al-Ḥujja Sayyid Hāshim al-Hāshimī, Sayyid al-Sīstānī discussed infallible guardianship in its three parts: legislative guardianship (*wilāya tashrīʿiyya*), procedural guardianship (*wilāya ijrāʾiyya*), and guardianship of promulgation (*wilāya tablīghiyya*). All these examples are proof of our scholars' mastery of the science of doctrine based on the infallible texts that contain information on the relevant issues, in addition to their encyclopedic knowledge of other domains.

This is why all our great *marājiʿ*, without exception, are skilled and perceptive experts in all the sciences that are relevant to determining legal rulings or Islamic concepts in any field. An example is when martyr al-Ṣadr concluded from the texts of the Qurʾān and the infallibles ﷺ that the economic problem is neither due to a lack of natural resources nor due to the inconsistency between production and distribution. The economic problem is due to the incompatibility between the instinct of ownership and public interest. The theory of Islam allows individual ownership not absolutely but as a way to achieve public interest. Similarly, Āyatullāh Jaʿfar al-Subḥānī deduced the existence of the unconscious (*al-ʿaql al-bāṭin*) from the narrations of Imām ʿAlī ﷺ, and the Sayyid of the sect,

Imām al-Khū'ī ⚕, deduced many Islamic concepts from the noble texts. Among these concepts is his discussion of dissimulation (*taqiyya*) in his *Tanqīḥ*, stating that the might of the religion is related to the might of its leaders, which is incompatible with the leader doing something that causes the weakness or the humiliation of the religion. This is why al-Ṣādiq ⚕ said, "I never practice dissimulation regarding three things: drinking intoxicants (*al-muskir*), wiping the socks [during ablution] (*mash al-khuffayn*), and temporary marriage (*mut'a*) during the pilgrimage."

Another example is Imām al-Khū'ī's ⚕ philosophical conclusion based on the philosophers' opinion that the soul (*al-nafs*) belongs to the category of abstracts (*mujarradāt*) because it is indivisible. Imām al-Khū'ī ⚕ said that matter (*māddiyyāt*) is of two types: matter that has a body (*jurm*), which is divisible, and matter that don't have a body, like the energy resulting from matter, which is indivisible except in the imagination (*wahm*). Based on the noble texts, Imām al-Khū'ī ⚕ concluded that the soul is not an absolute abstract.

In *Kitāb al-Qaḍā'* and other books of his, Imām al-Khū'ī ⚕ said that there is a matter proven by reason and textual evidence (*al-'aql wal-naql*), and it is the necessity of maintaining order. Order is necessary to preserve life, dignity, and money. A branch of this principle, which belongs to sociology, is the prohibition (*ḥurma*) of disobeying order and the guardianship of the jurist over the maintenance of order. Another example is his idea at the economical level that energy falls under the category of public wealth that cannot be among the possessions of the individual. The individual simply has the right of lien (*ḥaqq al-ikhtiṣāṣ*) under the headline of acquisitive prescription (*ḥiyāza*) and other such categories.

If the jurist wanted to specify a legal ruling in the domain of acts of worship (*ʿibādāt*), transactions (*muʿāmalāt*), or public or private relations, he should go back to the Qur'ān, the Prophetic texts, or the texts of Ahl al-Bayt ﷺ. The same applies when defining Islamic concepts in the fields of psychology, sociology, management, and economics. Deducing legal rulings or Islamic concept from these texts requires several branches of knowledge such as language (*ʿilm al-lugha*), logic (*ʿilm al-manṭiq*), rhetoric (*ʿilm al-balāgha*), jurisprudence, and, in some cases, the science of transmitters (*ʿilm al-rijāl*).

For this reason, a person cannot attain the level of jurist until he becomes a professional and an expert in these sciences. In addition, attaining the sound opinion in many juristic and legal issues can only be done if the jurist was familiar with philosophy and had the full ability to evaluate philosophical theories and accept or critique them. To clarify this issue, we will discuss a point which is jurisprudence and philosophy. There is an idea that philosophy is necessarily related to authenticating Islamic thought at the level of general concepts, jurisprudence, and deducing legal rulings. This is because philosophy is the science that discusses existence and the existent inasmuch as it is existent (*al-mawjūd bi-mā huwa mawjūd*). In other words, philosophy is the science that discusses objective truths, which makes every other science inherently in need of it. However, this statement deserves consideration for two reasons.

First, we undoubtedly need to refer to ideological concepts of the principles of jurisprudence, such as monotheism, prophethood, and the Day of Return, to intellectual discussions. When comparing religious thought and Western intellectual schools, we need intellectual discussions based on accuracy and precision. This applies to epistemology (*naẓariyyat al-maʿrifa*), the meaning of the soul, the logical proof of syllogism (*bāb al-qiyās*), the mathematical proof of probability, and formulating concepts in the fields of ethics, education, psychology, sociology, and others.

This sometimes requires going back to philosophical discussions and rules, not for the sake of philosophy itself but in order to be able to formulate these intellectual points in a philosophical way. Philosophical rules are like a formal cause (*ʿilla ṣuwariyya*); as for the material cause (*ʿilla māddiyya*), it is a result of reason and its accuracy. Philosophical rules may provide answers to some misconceptions regarding monotheism and justice. However, refuting misconceptions does not rely exclusively on philosophical rules. To clarify this further, we say that philosophy is not a science whose theories are absolutely certain, making it a yardstick for other sciences. Philosophy is not inherent to jurisprudence such that a scholar who is not a philosopher would not be a jurist. To prove that, we mention a number of points.

First, philosophy is not like mathematics in that every inference inherently requires it. The science of mathematics is based on intuitive, undeniable conclusions, whereas philosophy inherently involves debating in many of its topics, such as the precedence of essence (*māhiyya*) or existence and the discussion of whether existence is composed of several realities or one gradational reality (*ḥaqīqa mushakkaka*). Another example is whether copulative existence (*al-wujūd al-rābiṭ*) is based in reality or not and whether an accident (*'araḍ*) has independent existence (*wujūd nafsī*) aside from the existence of the essence (*al-jawhar*).

Logic is also like this in some of its theories. In logic, the empirical proof (*dalīl tajrībī*) that is based on induction (*istiqrā'*) depends on the suppressed premise (*muqaddima maṭwiyya*) that coincidental matters (*al-ittifāqī*) are not permanent or most probable (*laysa dā'imiyyan wa-lā akhthariyyan*). Another example is that similar things are the same in regards to what applies and doesn't apply to them. For this reason, empirical propositions are necessary propositions (*qaḍāya ḍarūriyya*). In his *al-Usus al-Manṭiqiyya Lil-Istiqrā'*, martyr al-Ṣadr ؒ denied this rational premise (*muqaddima 'aqliyya*), stating that the consequence of each experience may be related to a specific reason and relating the proof of induction to probability.

Second, some scholars of jurisprudence have criticized certain philosophical concepts, such as the comprehensiveness of the rule that from One only one emerges (*al-wāḥid lā yaṣdur minhu illā wāḥid*). Sayyid al-Khū'ī ؒ questioned this and said that there is a difference between a natural cause (*al-'illa al-ṭabī'iyya*) and a willing agent (*al-fā'il al-mukhtār*), stating that the rule does not include the latter as a subject. Another example is the issue of the world's eternity (*qidam*), in which its posteriority (*ta'akhkhur*) to God ﷻ is gradational and not temporal based on the rule that the cause and effect happen at the same time but differ in degree. Many of the scholars of our time considered this an explicit contradiction of the texts that indicate that the world is created in time.

Another example is the rule that a thing does not exist if it is not necessary. The philosophers generalized this rule to include voluntary action, whereas Sayyid martyr al-Ṣadr ؒ said in his *Uṣūl* that if this rule includes voluntary action, this negates the action's voluntariness because voluntariness means the soul's authority of choosing the existence or non-existence of an action.

Another example, also from martyr al-Ṣadr's ﷺ *Uṣūl*, is when he said that the tablet of reality is more comprehensive than the tablet of existence, which apparently opposes the concept of the principality of existence (*aṣālat al-wujūd*). All these are clear proofs that the relation of philosophy to the structure of jurisprudence is debatable. Someone who refuses to rely on philosophy is basing himself on some essential discussions of certain philosophical theories, and his refusal is not because he has failed to understand philosophy.

Third, all our past scholars, such as al-Mufīd ﷺ, al-Murtaḍā ﷺ, al-Shaykh al-Ṭūsī ﷺ, and others, engaged in theological discussions on justice, prophethood, and Imāmate, proposing brilliant intellectual points. Examples are al-Murtaḍā's ﷺ *al-Shāfī fil-Imām* and *Tanzīh al-Anbiyā'*. None of these scholars relied on philosophy at all. This emphasizes that the need for intellectual themes in rectifying proofs is one thing, and the need for philosophical rules is another thing entirely.

Fourth, many philosophical theories are external or supplementary to theological discussions, which means that they cannot be a methodology in legal and jurisprudential proofs. For example, when we consider the methodology of al-Muḥaqqiq Muḥammad Ḥusayn al-Iṣfahānī ﷺ in jurisprudence, we notice that he integrated philosophical theories into his proofs. Although he is a master of philosophy, this did not cause a radical change in his methodology; it added certain points of formulation to his discussion or provided some additions that the proof itself did not depend on.

To give the example of the prayer of travelers (*ṣalāt al-musāfir*), the following secondary consideration is proposed. If the religiously accountable person was riding a usurped car (*maghṣūba*), this would not require him to perform complete prayers (*tamām*). The secret behind that is the customary (*ʿurf*) formulation mentioned in Sayyid al-Khūʾī's ﷺ *Mustanad al-ʿUrwa*, which states that the definition of travel (*safar*) is being away from one's homeland (*waṭan*). Unless being away from one's homeland is prohibited because it involves a prohibited component, such as casting oneself into destruction (*al-ilqāʾ fil-tahluka*) or performing a prohibited thing, complete prayers would not be required.

In the above example, being away from one's homeland is neither prohibited in itself nor done for prohibited purposes. The prohibited aspect is a complementary thing, which is riding that car. Custom (*ʿurf*) differentiates between travel itself and the means of transportation used to travel. For this reason, a prohibited act, i.e. getting into a usurped car, may be committed without actually traveling, and the opposite is true. Meanwhile, on page 70 of his *Ṣalāt al-Musāfir*, al-Muḥaqqiq al-Iṣfahānī قدس سره formulated the issue in a philosophical way, speaking of three things.

The first thing constitutes the relative universes that the traveler comprises. The second thing constitutes the relative universes that the animal (*al-dābba*) comprises. The third thing is riding the animal, which belongs to the category of possession (*maqūlāt al-jida*). Categories differ in their existence and essence. This inevitably means that this person's trip cannot fall under the headline of usurpation or be a preliminary to it. The usurpation itself is a preliminary to the trip, which means that performing complete prayers is not required in this case. Another example is a secondary discussion related to leasing (*ijāra*). The famous definition of leasing is that it is giving possession of something in exchange for a return (*tamlīk al-manfaʿa bi-awaḍ*). Al-Muḥaqqiq al-Ṭihrānī قدس سره objects to this definition because residing in a house (*al-suknā*), for instance, is an accident (*ʿaraḍ*) and one of the tenant's actions; it is not one of the house's attributes (*ṣifāt*). For this reason, the landlord does not own the residency because it is an action of someone other than himself. If the landlord does not own the residency, how can he give the tenant possession of it?

Scholars have responded to this, for example in *Mustanad al-ʿUrwa*, by saying that the landlord gives the tenant possession not of the actual residency itself, but of the house's customary capability (*qābiliyya*

ʿurfiyya) of being resided in. Capability is one of the house's attributes, which means that capability is owned as a consequence of owning the house. Al-Muḥaqqiq al-Iṣfahānī ﵀ gave a philosophical formulation of this answer in his *Kitāb al-Ijāra*. He said that residing in the house is a principle under the headline of residency in the house (*sākiniyya*) and inhabitancy of the house (*maskūniyya*) because they are correlated (*mutaḍāyifān*). The context of inhabitancy is one of the house's affairs, not the context of residency. It may be said that residing means being within the house, which makes it a relative accident (*min al- aʿrāḍ al-nisbiyya*). A relative accident is related to its subject, which is the person residing in the house in the example, as well as to its possessive construction (*ṭaraf al-iḍāfa*), which is the house in the example. Based on this latter relation, the possession of the house is valid.

These and other examples are proof that philosophy is greatly integrated in formulations and that it adds some points that are part of the principles of jurisprudence. This applies to Islamic concepts as well. When we consider the doctrinal rule of the position between the two positions (*al-amr bayn al-amrayn*), we approach it from two angles. From one angle, we say that a person's action requires two elements: willpower (*irāda*) and the ability of acting (*al-qudra ʿalā al-ījād*). Although the first element depends on the human being, the second depends on God. This means that an action is neither entirely voluntary (*ikhtiyārī*) nor entirely predestined (*jabrī*); it occupies an in-between position. This is a general formulation of the principle of the position between the two positions.

From another angle, we say that the occurrence of the action requires being entailed by something (*al-muqtaḍī*) which gives it its existence, and it requires a condition (*sharṭ*), which actuates its existence (*fiʿliyyat al-wujūd*). Divine aid (*al-madad al-ilāhī*) is the thing that entails the action's existence because the effect (*al-maʿlūl*), in all of its branches, including the action, inherently needs its cause to exist and persist (*ḥudūthan wa-baqāʾan*). The condition of the action is the human being's choice and will. Since the thing that entails the existence of a person's action is external to him, his action is not purely by choice, and since the action depends on the person's choice, his action is not purely forced. It is an in-between position. This is the philosophical formulation of this truth.

Another example is this. In the discussion of prophethood, it is said that performing a miracle is proof of the truth of the claim of prophecy. This proof is formulated in the books of theology along the following lines. Providing a liar with a miracle is reprehensible (*qabīḥ*) because it encourages ignorance (*ighrāʾ bil-jahl*). For this reason, the miracle worker should be someone honest. The philosophical formulation of this proof is that the ability to perform miracles is a delegation from the world of command

(*ʿalam al-amr*). Delegation requires the connection between the world of command and the world of creation (*ʿalam al-khalq*) based on the congruence (*sinkhiyya*) of the effect and the cause. This means that performing miracles is a proof of prophethood.

The above shows that philosophy is often integrated into theological, legal, or jurisprudential discussions, and it adds certain points to them. However, it does not imply a change in the knowledge itself such that a jurist or theologian should be required to be a philosopher.

The jurist's actual need for philosophy is for two reasons. The first reason is understanding philosophical terms. Many philosophical terms are repeated by the scholars of jurisprudence. Examples include the difference between the categories of predication (*al-ḥaml*), the essential (*al-dhātī*), and the accident, the difference between the kinds of intelligibles (*al-maʿqūl*), and the difference between simplicity (*al-basāṭa*) and compoundedness (*al-tarkīb*). Other examples are the phrase that the essential is not caused (*al-dhātī lā yuʿallal*), the categories of opposition (*aqsām al-taqābul*), the parts of the cause, the category of condition (*maqūlat al-sharṭ*), the kinds of necessary concomitants (*al-lāzim*), and simple making (*al-jaʿl al-*

basīṭ) and composite making (*al-jaʿl al-taʾlīfī*).[18] Understanding these terms and using them correctly only requires a general familiarity with philosophy, without the need of becoming an expert in it.

What if someone asks, "Have the jurists ever mixed up these terms used, and explained them incorrectly in a way that shows that they are not familiar with philosophy but simply inherited it from their predecessors?"

The answer is that whoever reviews the answers of our jurists, and especially Sayyid al-Khūʾī ﷷ, will find that they know these terms precisely, both at the level of concepts and application. An example is that Sayyid al-Khūʾī ﷷ states, concerning the issue of opposites, that there is no real opposition between conceptual existents (*iʿtibāriyyāt*); the opposition is either at the beginning or the end. About the statement that everything connected to something of prior rank (*mutaqaddim rutbatan*) is itself of prior rank, Sayyid al-Khūʾī ﷷ says that priority (*al-taqaddum al-rutabī*) is of two types, passive and active. The latter type requires something that entails it. He also says that the impossibility of a posterior condition (*al-sharṭ al-mutaʾakhkhir*) is based

[18] Translator's note: "The meaning of 'making' (*jaʿl*) is the acting of a cause, or, in other words, the real effect of something which makes an effect or is effective." See Mahdī Ḥāʾirī Yazdī, *Universal Science: An Introduction to Islamic Metaphysics*, trans. John Cooper, 115.

on the application of the rulings of the world of creation (*ʿālam al-takwīn*) to the conceptual world (*ʿālam al-iʿtibār*).

On the topic of unificational (*ittiḥādī*) or annexational (*inḍImāmī*) composition, Sayyid al-Khūʾī ﷺ says that unified composition is conceived of as an abstracted entity (*al-umūr al-intizāʿiyya*) because abstract entities exist when the origin of their extraction exists. An example is the existence of the attribute (*al-maqbūl*) with the existence of the recipient subject (*al-qābil*). For this reason, their external existence (*al-wujūd al-khārijī*) is one and the same; two actual existents cannot be united as one. There are other examples in the works of Sayyid al-Khūʾī ﷺ and his students which show their intimate knowledge of philosophical terms.

The second reason for the jurist's actual need for philosophy is that the derivation (*istinbāṭ*) [of the ruling] depends on it. By induction (*istiqrāʾ*), we have not found a ruling in jurisprudence whose derivation depends on a philosophical principle except rarely or partially. For example, in the discussion of the combination of commands and prohibitions (*ijtimāʿ al-amr wal nahī*), the question is whether their combination is unificational or annexational. This is a minor premise that has a certain result because certain opinions state that it is impossible for commanding and forbidding to combine in one external entity. An example is this. When commanding something implies forbidding its opposite, the discussion here is about the intellectual possibility of opposition between legal rulings based on the fact that a ruling concerns the soul's will (*irāda*) and aversion *(karāha)*, regardless of the opposition's beginning and ending.

Other examples include the discussion about the principality of existence or essence when addressing the continuance (*istiṣḥāb*) of pre-eternal nonexistence (*'adam azalī*). The question is about the difference between accepting the continuance of the concomitants of existence (*lawāzim al-wujūd*) or the concomitance of the essence (*lawāzim al-māhiyya*). Another example is the rule that from One only one emerges when discussing the concept of the condition.

Some may think that these are philosophical themes, such as the discussion of the truth of the will and the truth of the in-between position in regards to the unity of the aim (*ṭalab*) and the will (*irāda*). In truth, these are theological discussions. They are mentioned in the principles of jurisprudence by way of digression and not because deriving the Lawgiver's meaning depends on them.

Other themes that may be thought to be philosophical are the necessity of discussing the value of rational evidence (*al-dalīl al-aqlī*), the value of definitiveness in proofs (*al-qaṭ' fī maqām al-istidlāl*), the rational intelligibility of good and bad (*al-ḥusn wal-qubḥ al-*

'aqliyyayn). However, these are theological discussions that are discussed as part of doctrine, not philosophy. These different examples emphasize one clear truth, which is that all of our *marāji'* and jurists have a say in correcting philosophical opinions. We can conclude three things; the first is about the position of being most learned (*a'lamiyya*). Being most learned is the ability to determine the legal ruling or the Islamic concept in any domain. This ability is based on three factors. The first factor is being skilled, having mastery in all the sciences that have to do with determining the position of the law, and being able to assess different theories and accept or reject them. This includes philosophical and theological theories that have to do with determining the legal ruling, even if the jurist is not a philosopher. The more intelligent a jurist is, the more skilled he will be in assessing and applying these theories and determining their relation to the ruling.

The conclusion is that the position of being most learned doesn't involve being skilled in Arabic grammar (*'ilm al-naḥw*), rhetoric, logic, philosophy, and other sciences that have to do with deriving the legal ruling. The most important thing about superior knowledge is the ability of the jurist to critique any theory within these sciences if it has to do with deriving the legal ruling. However, the jurist has to be a specialist in the theories of the principles of jurisprudence, which exclusively relate to deriving the legal ruling.

The second factor is having fine understanding and a good reputation, such that the jurist's understanding of the narrations and Qur'ānic texts is related to custom and the rules of language. The more perceptive and refined a jurist is, and the more familiar he is with the customs within the texts, the better his understanding will be. The third factor is being experienced in the narrations of Ahl al-Bayt ﷺ, including their chains of transmission and content, in addition to being experienced in the books of *ḥadīth*, *rijāl*, and language. The older a jurist gets while continuing to do research, the more experienced he will be. Determining the concept of being most learned and the factors relevant to it is not subject to disagreement in the seminary and there are no different opinions about it. This concept is similar to the concepts of *ijtihād* and *faqāha* in that our jurists do not differ about determining it and the factors related to it.

As for absolute learnedness (*aʿlamiyya muṭlaqa*) sometimes it means the most knowledgeable and the most experienced in jurisprudence and theology, i.e. the science of doctrine. There is no proof of this position, as it involves two specialties: jurisprudence and theology. There is no proof that the authority (*ḥujjiyat*) of the jurist's opinion in the former requires his mastery of the latter although they treat different subjects.

The narrations that praise the jurists as the trustees of the apostles, the inheritors of the prophets, and the strongholds of Islam only praise the jurists at these levels. They do not prove the superiority of the most learned jurist's opinion when there is a disagreement among the jurists. Another opinion is that the most learned is the jurist who is the best in all the sciences that are involved in legal derivation, such that the jurist in question is the most capable in the domains that have to do with religious thought. However, this cannot be the case of any jurist based on the nature of the human lifespan, and it has not happened since the time of our Imāms ﷺ. Just like no one can be the most learned in all medical specialties in our age because each specialty requires a lifetime of practice, the jurist cannot be the best in all the sciences that are even remotely related to religious thought.

In his book *al-Tajdīd wal-Ijtihād fil-Islām*, martyr Muṭahharī ؒ says, by quoting Shaykh ʿAbd al-Karīm al-Yazdī al-Ḥā'irī ؒ, that our times call for specialization such that each jurist would be a *marjaʿ* in a specific branch because he is specialized in it. This is because the science of jurisprudence is diverse, and its themes and questions are many. This means that Muṭahharī ؒ believes that comprehensive *Marjiʿiyyah* is not compatible with the age. If we say that most learnedness includes the knowledge in philosophy and theology as well, we might as well include the best knowledge (*al-aqwā'iyya*) in psychology, sociology, and law because they sometimes have to do with analyzing the rational principles and the meanings of the texts. After all, all these sciences are in some way related to understanding and analyzing a text. This means that we should either consider having the best knowledge in all the sciences part of being most learned or we should say that those sciences are unrelated. As for making distinctions by saying philosophy and mysticism (*ʿirfān*) are related to understanding and analyzing the texts but the other sciences are not, it doesn't make sense.

This raises several questions. The first is this. Jurists have different methodologies; some have a methodology based on philosophy, like al-Muḥaqqiq al-Iṣfahānī ﵀, and others have a methodology based on custom like Imām al-Ḥakīm ﵀. The implication of this is that the status of most learnedness cannot be determined. If the methodologies are different, how could one of them be classified as most learned? The answer is that there isn't a methodological difference among the jurists. A methodology constitutes information that affects most legal issues, but this isn't the case. Philosophy or theology, for instance, only affect some issues and not most of them. Such a limited influence doesn't constitute a methodology.

Secondly, the philosophical methodology of al-Muḥaqqiq al-Iṣfahānī ﵀ in the principles of jurisprudence did not create a radical change in the principles of jurisprudence but simply added a philosophical flavor to them. It did not cause a radical and fundamental change. An example is the concept of the condition in the principles of jurisprudence. God says if (*idhā*) the slaughtered animal's (*dhabīḥa*) eyes flutter, you can eat from it (*fa-kul minhā*). This sentence involves the concept of conditionality whose point is that if the animal's eyes don't flutter upon slaughter, it should not be eaten. Proving this concept can be done through language by saying that the conditional particle (*adāt al-sharṭ*) *idhā* was used to suspend the consequence (*al-jazāʾ*). The eating (*fa-kul*) is based on the condition "if the slaughtered animal's eyes flutter." This means the eating is negated if the condition is negated.

Another way to prove this concept is based on the customs of the principles of jurisprudence. This is by saying that the conditional sentence implies that the condition is the cause of the consequence. Making a condition means that the cause is restricted to the consequence, which means that the consequence is negated when the condition is negated. There is also a philosophical proof which states that the consequence, i.e. the permissibility of eating the animal, may have several causes such as eye movement, falling from a height, or crashing into a boulder. This would require the presence of several causes in bringing about one effect (*maʿlūl*), which is impossible based on the concept that the one rationally cannot depend on the many. If it is valid that the consequence has one cause instead, which applies to our sentence, this implies the negation of the consequence with the negation of the condition. This is what we had already said, which means that the philosophical methodology does not cause an essential change in the principles of jurisprudence; it only adds some details.

Linguistic details and discussions within the principles of jurisprudence, such as derivatives (*al-mushtaqqāt*) and imperatives, don't cause an essential change, and the same applies to philosophical details and discussions. Even if the use of philosophy becomes a partial methodology within the science of the principles of jurisprudence, it doesn't change the science itself. This applies to jurisprudence and the principles of jurisprudence. For this reason, the method doesn't affect determining the capacity of *faqāha* or *afqahiyya*.

The second question is this. What is the proof of the relation between being most learned and the authority of the jurist's legal decree? The answer is that if we go back to the opinion of rational society, we see that if experts differ about something, rational people follow the opinion of the one who is most experienced and precise. For example, if doctors differed about the diagnosis of an illness or the prescription of a medicine, a rational person would listen to the most experienced and precise doctor. This rational custom was not forbidden by the sacred Lawgiver but rather approved by Him ﷻ. This custom is proof that if the jurists differed about a ruling, the opinion of the most learned should be followed. The most learned jurist's legal decree is certainly authoritative, in that following it is an excuse before God ﷻ. However, the authoritativeness of the decrees of other jurists when there is a difference of opinion is doubtable, so following them is not definitively an excuse before God ﷻ. Applying continuance to the concept of the lack of authoritativeness implies that the latter's legal decree is not authoritative.

Third, a person's object (*maṭlūb*) is of two kinds: his object is either to reach the reality of a situation (*taḥṣīl al-waqiʿ*) or to absolve himself of liability (*ibrāʾ al-dhimma*). When rational people choose to adopt the opinion of the most learned person, this belongs to the first category. For example, if a person wanted to treat his illness, his object is to match the reality of the situation through the diagnosis of a physician. For this reason, if the physicians differ in their diagnosis, the opinion of the most learned among them is followed. A person's object, however, also could be to absolve himself of liability, as in the case of jurisprudence. The religiously accountable person cannot reach the actual ruling (*al-ḥukm al-wāqiʿī*), so his object is to absolve himself of liability before God ﷻ. In this case, there are no proofs supporting the view that rational people rely on the opinion of the most learned person exclusively.

The answer to that involves two elements. The first element is that the most important thing required of the religiously accountable person in the domain of legal rulings is reaching the reality of a situation if it is indeed reachable. This is because all religious obligations and rulings were legislated to achieve important benefits and prevent corruption in human society. Since the purpose of legislating rulings is preserving the actual domain of benefits and preventing corruption, what is required of the religiously accountable person is reaching the actual ruling in order to preserve its domain. Since the path to achieving that requires consideration and *ijtihad*, the jurist is the person who takes it upon himself to exercise the highest degrees of effort in order to determine the reality of the situation.

The way to achieve this is limited to the texts of the Book and the *sunnah*. Most of the legal rulings that God ﷻ revealed to His Prophet ﷺ are contained in the verses and the narrations of the infallibles ﷺ. The jurist's role is to reach the actual rulings contained in those texts using a variety of epistemological tools (*al-adawāt al-maʿrifiyya*) such as language, logic, the principles of jurisprudence, and so on, in order to reach reality, which is made of the legal rulings contained in the Book or the *sunnah*. The more experienced a jurist is in these texts and the more precise he is in using these rational epistemological tools to determine the definite purpose of the texts, the closer his opinion will be to reality.

For this reason, when rational people agree to follow the opinion of the most learned when the professionals in any domain differ, this includes the difference among jurists in determining the purpose of the texts because it is an example of seeking to reach the reality of the situation.

The second element is that when the texts do not contain an obvious proof of the legal ruling, it is the jurist's duty to determine the practical action to be taken when in doubt. In this case, the status of being most learned is of great importance. The purpose of determining the practical action is to ensure being excusable before God ﷻ. The more precise a jurist is in determining the action, the more certainty his opinion would involve and be excusable before God ﷻ.

Fourth, the most learned person to whom rational people refer when there is disagreement is the person whose opinion most closely reaches reality. This may be known in sensory and experimental cases, such as in medicine. Knowing the most experienced physician is achieved through experience and the observation that this physician's opinion agrees with reality in most cases. If the reality of a situation cannot be known in a certain domain, how can we determine the most learned person?

This is the problem about determining the most learned jurist. There are cases where we don't know what the reality is in order to determine the jurist who is closest to it. The answer to this is what follows. First, we mentioned that the religious reality is the group of rulings that came from the Sacred Lawgiver. The way for reaching religious reality is to examine the texts of the Qurʾān and the *ḥadīths*. Since the Lawgiver expressed the rulings in the texts in the same way that is customary, reaching the reality of a ruling by examining the text is done in the same way of reaching any customary conclusion through examining the words said about it.

For this reason, the closest methodology to reality may be determined by considering the tools used for clarifying and explaining the texts. There are epistemological tools used by rational society and Arab custom in determining the meanings of the theologians. If rational experience states that these tools allow us to come as close as possible to reality because they achieve people's actual purposes in most domains, these same tools may be used to determine the purpose of the Islamic Lawgiver.

For example, if a king, president, poet, or teacher speaks about a certain thing, the way of knowing his actual purpose is to use linguistic tools and customary proofs in order to determine his meaning. This same way is used to determine the actual ruling and the real purpose of Islam within the texts containing the rulings since the Sacred Lawgiver did not prevent this rational way. For example, people may differ about the meaning of the President's words. In this case, the person most knowledgeable about the President's way of speaking and most capable of using certain tools to determine his meaning should be referred back to. The same thing applies in the case of the Lawgiver.

For this reason, the more precise the jurist is in using these tools and determining their areas of application, the closer his effort and legal derivation will be to reality, which amounts to pursuing the purpose of the sacred Lawgiver. The experience that rational people use to determine the most learned speakers among presidents and poets and so on applies identically to the most learned jurist in religious rulings. Second, determining reality is not limited to sensory empirical methods; it may be done using knowledge and rules that have been definitively proved. The human intellect observes the relation between a proven fact and reality. The importance of such a fact is that it matches reality, even if there is no sensory experience that proves the truth of this fact. For example, let's assume that we don't know whether Imāmate and infallibility are related or not. Such a fact is judged as true and conforming to reality not through experience but through definitive proof. The same applies to legal rulings.

Determining the reality of the codified rules of jurisprudence and its principles that are definitively proved is based on this proof. The more precise a jurist is in determining and applying these rules, the most learned and the closest to reality he would be.

Undoubtedly, determining the most learned jurist is particularly easy in our time for the experts, i.e. the *mujtahids* and teachers in the seminary. This is due to the availability of the means of communication in our time, the dissemination of research, and the ability of accessing the lessons of all the jurists whose books and opinions are known among the virtuous. This makes it easier to determine the most learned jurist.

The Jurist and Exegesis

A person who is skilled in language, rhetoric, theology, and the principles of religion will also be skilled in the science of exegesis. These sciences, which are the tools that the jurist uses to determine the religious ruling, are also used in the science of exegesis. It is unimaginable for a jurist not to be a Qurʾānic exegete. How can that be when the proofs of a large part of the rulings are contained in the noble Qurʾān? Examples include the verses on inheritance and the rulings on transactions.

Jurisprudence and exegesis are like inseparable twins in terms of methodology. You may observe this in our scholars' books of jurisprudence when they discuss a Qurʾānic verse. Interpreting the Noble Qurʾān may be done in more than one way. The first way is through the Book itself using other verses that discuss the same topic even if they were in other *sūras*. Another way is through the context of the verses that spoke about the same thing and were revealed at the same time. Another way is to rely on intuitive reasonable judgments and rational principles as they are relevant to the Qurʾānic text. Another way is using linguistic rules and customary proofs, or using explanatory narrations. Using these same tools and this same methodology, the jurist understands the rulings in the noble verses and in the narrations of the infallibles ﷺ.

It's true that the jurist may not have the time to interpret the Qurʾān from cover to cover and that he may not be experienced about the totality of the Qurʾān's contents, but this does not make him any less of an exegete. He has all the tools and elements required of an exegete.

The Scholarly History of Our Jurists

The skill of our past and contemporary *marājiʿ* in all the various sciences of the seminary is an undoubtable and an undeniable truth. Imām Khomeini ﷺ wrote on jurisprudence, the principles of jurisprudence, mysticism, and ethics, and he presented many philosophical opinions in his books on the principles of jurisprudence. His students walked in his footsteps regarding this variety and multiplicity of skills, as it is well-known. Our Sayyid al-Khūʾī ﷺ, the teacher of the jurists and *mujtahids*, and his students represent a comprehensive school of knowledge.

Sayyid al-Khū'ī ﷺ wrote *al-Bayān* in the field of exegesis, *Naẓariyyat al-Amr Bayn al-Amrayn* in the field of doctrine, and *Nafaḥāt al-I'jāz*, and he wrote on the truth of divine will in his discussion of the unity of the aim and the will as part of the principles of jurisprudence. Sayyid al-Khū'ī ﷺ also spoke with rhetorical and linguistic skill and discernment about the verse of guardianship in the fifth part of his lectures. He also spoke about the verse "He said, 'I am making you the Imām of mankind.' Said he, 'And from among my descendants?' He said, 'My pledge does not extend to the unjust'"[19] in his discussion of derivatives as part of the principles of jurisprudence. This indicates a special brilliance in the sciences of rhetoric and language. The absence of a single book that combines these doctrinal discussions that are present in Sayyid al-Khū'ī's ﷺ different books on the principles of jurisprudence does not negate his mastery and skill in theology. Shaykh Ibrāhīm al-Khazrajī thankfully combined these doctrinal points in a book he titled *Buḥūth 'Aqā'idiyya Lil-Sayyid al-Khū'ī*, and 'Allāma Shaykh Ibrāhīm al-Nuṣayrāwī thankfully explained and published Sayyid al-Khū'ī's ﷺ doctrinal system.

Sayyid al-Khū'ī ﷺ also displayed skill in philosophy by discussing philosophical theories within the science of jurisprudence such as the theory that from One only

---

[19] Sūrat al-Baqara, verse 124.

one emerges, the theory that the Creator's precedence over the created is the cause's precedence over the effect (*taqaddum al-khāliq ʿalā al-makhlūq taqaddum al-ʿilla ʿalā al-maʿlūl*), and theory of the abstractness of the human soul (*tajarrud al-nafs al-insāniyya*). He also displayed skill in the rational sciences when discussing the posterior condition and hierarchy (*al-tarattub*), in addition to the masterful work he's done in the science of transmitters in his book *Muʿjam Rijāl al-ḥadīth.*

His students include the teacher in the blessed seminary in Qum, Shaykh al-Waḥīd al-Khurāsānī, whose encyclopedic knowledge and philosophical skill are displayed in *al-Ḥaqq al-Mubīn* and *Muqṭatafāt Walāʾiyya.* Shaykh al-Khurāsānī's work in the principles of jurisprudence include many of his theories of Qurʾānic exegesis, theology, and language. Another one of his students is the jurist of his age Shaykh al-Tabrīzī ﵀ who has compressive knowledge of all the sciences that have to do with determining religious rulings in his books on jurisprudence and its principles. His knowledge is also vast in the fields of theology and exegesis, as evidenced by his book on doctrinal issues *al-Anwār al-Ilāhiyya*. The expert jurist Sayyid Muḥammad Saʿīd al-Ḥakīm ﵀ also has vast knowledge in language, theology, exegesis, and *ḥadīth*, which is evident in his books *Fī Riḥāb al-ʿAqīda* and *Uṣūl al-ʿAqīda*.

The seminary contains many other examples, and one of the most important of them is the sacred Sayyid and the guided divine light who is a great scholar of exegesis, jurisprudence, philosophy, and mysticism, i.e. Sayyid al-Sabziwārī قدس سره. This is apparent in Sayyid al-Sabziwārī's قدس سره two books, *Muhadhdhib al-Aḥkām* and *Mawāhib al-Raḥmān Fī Tafsīr al-Qur'ān*. Additional examples include other scholars of the seminary and the chosen elite of the contemporary *marājiʿ* of the Shīʿa in Iran, Iraq, and elsewhere, may God preserve them all.

I mentioned some of my own teachers' output not because I wanted to limit these qualities to them, but to show that the *Marjiʿiyyah* in the scholarly seminaries in Najaf and Qum encompasses varied intellectual schools and represents the door to the knowledge of Ahl al-Bayt عليهم السلام, being an extension of the position of Imāmate in its scholars' sacred capabilities and divine talents.

The Purpose of the Sciences

The identity of each science depends on its purpose and the purpose of writing it down. The purpose of psychology is to analyze the self to enable it to keep its capabilities and vigor, and the purpose of philosophy is to analyze the truth of existence and the existent, while the purpose of the principles of jurisprudence is to establish the validity of the proofs used in religious knowledge. Lastly, the purpose of jurisprudence is investigating the legitimacy of any position and act and considering the relation of any concept to the sacred Law.

Hence the necessity of jurisprudence and its principles in the system of Islamic sciences. The science of the principles of jurisprudence, which proves the validity of the methods, isn't less important than the sciences that analyze knowledge itself, such as philosophy, theology, or mysticism. The same applies to the science of jurisprudence, which concerns itself with legitimacy. This is because all these sciences constitute the totality of Islamic sciences, regardless of whether they are methodological or analytical.

This is why we say that one of the main pillars of the position of *Marjiʿiyyah* is the science of jurisprudence, also known as the science of the lawful and the unlawful. It is a science no less difficult and deep than philosophy and theology, as its own experts testify. It is also not any less important than the science of doctrine. All these sciences are inseparable from one another. For example, unless we prove the authority of the infallible's عليه السلام words in theology, we cannot derive the religious ruling from the *ḥadīth* attributed to him عليه السلام. Similarly, unless we prove the impermissibility of attributing a certain legislation to the Lawgiver (*ḥurmat al-tashrīʿ*), the authority of confidence (*ḥujjiyyat iṭmiʾnān*), or the authority of a trustworthy transmitter's report, we would be unable to attribute many doctrinal concepts to the Lawgiver because their proof is transmitted.

Attributing concepts to the Lawgiver without proving the authority of a report or proving the authority of confidence constitutes unlawful legislation in the principles of jurisprudence.

Determining permissibility or impermissibility of emulation in doctrinal matters (*al-taqlīd fil-ʿaqāʾid*) requires the intervention of jurisprudence. Jurisprudence even interferes in ethics and Islamic culture more generally. Ethical concepts such as vanity, humility, and admitting one's mistakes may only be attributed to the sacred Law through jurisprudence. Other examples include women's position in Islam, animal rights, and some theories in the humanities, such as the unconscious within psychology, leadership within management, the relation between the means of production and distribution and the relation between private and public property in economics, and formulating any other Islamic concept at any field of the humanities. None of these concepts may be attributed to the sacred Law without the intervention of jurisprudence and its tools.

Determining the validity or invalidity of any concept in any field requires resorting to the religious texts and deriving rulings about this concept from them, and accepting or rejecting it. This is done using the tools of the principles of jurisprudence, language, the science of transmitters, and logic. Based on the results, it may be determined whether the concept may be attributed to the sacred Law or not. This is the methodology of jurisprudence, which is involved in all fields. Even in politics, determining the legitimacy of any political position within the *umma*, or between states, depends on the judgment of jurisprudence as lawful or unlawful and legitimate or illegitimate. This emphasizes the influence of jurisprudence in all fields, which means it is like the backbone of Islamic thought, as it comprises no less than 70% of the total of Islamic thought.

There are concepts that fall under the headline of etiquette and knowledge. There are concepts that relate to Islam in their capacity as legal rulings but whose content falls under etiquette, doctrine, or general Islamic concepts. The absolute necessity of the science of jurisprudence does not cancel the need for the other sciences that are used to consider and analyze Islamic sciences, such as psychology, sociology, and philosophy. Using philosophy and sociology to analyze knowledge after demonstrably proving their theories is no less important than philosophy itself as a science.

The conclusion is that jurisprudence in the epistemological system of religion is like the pillar of the sacred Law. This is especially true in the case of the jurisprudence of transactions within Islamic economics, which is fit to be a rule for day-to-day life. Jurisprudence is not limited to acts of worship; it also contains rulings on economic phenomena. If you go back to the relevant books, such as martyr al-Ṣadr's ﵀ *Iqtiṣādunā*, you will find that the transactions of Islamic jurisprudence constitute an entire system in their three elements: the philosophy of economics, the economic school, and the specific rules. These elements encompass the economic sphere, which means that the jurisprudence of what is lawful and unlawful is also a comprehensive economic system. This is why martyr al-Ṣadr ﴿ said the following about jurisprudence:

"The terms 'lawful' and 'unlawful' in Islam are a manifestation of the values and ideals of Islam. The natural conclusion behind this is achieving certainty about the existence of an Islamic economic school because the concept of lawful and unlawful extends to all human activities and behaviors in Islam. This includes the behavior of the ruler and the subjects, the seller and the buyer, the employer and the employee, and the employed and the unemployed. Every unit of behavior is either lawful or unlawful, which means that it is either just or unjust. If Islam includes a text that prohibits a certain positive or negative behavior, this behavior is unlawful. Otherwise, this behavior is lawful. If all the domains of economic life are subject to the categories of 'lawful' and 'unlawful' with their values and ideals, research about Islam would lead us to thinking about deducing and determining the economic school that is expressed by the categories of 'lawful' and 'unlawful' in their values, ideals, and concepts."[20]

One of the proofs of this is that *al-Kāfī*, which is the most important *ḥadīth* book containing the sayings of the infallibles 🕮, consists of eight volumes. Two of these volumes are on doctrine and general concepts and six are about the knowledge of the lawful and the unlawful. Most of the Imāms' 🕮 *ḥadīths* in the certified books of our ancient scholars are about determining the lawful and the unlawful, such as in the four books, *Wasā'il al-Shī'a*, and other sources. Most of the narrations that discussed scholars and the position of leadership focused on the necessity and importance of the knowledge of the lawful and the unlawful. For example, in the accepted narration of 'Umar ibn Ḥanẓala, Imām al-Ṣādiq 🕮 said, "Let them look to those of you who have narrated our *ḥadīths*, considered our *ḥalāl* and *ḥarām*, and known our rulings, and let them be content with those people as arbiters. I have made such a person the ruler over you." The narration from Imām al-Ḥusayn 🕮 states: "The course of matters and rulings should be conducted by those who know God and who are trustworthy about His *ḥalāl* and *ḥarām*."

This is why the *marja'* does not suffice himself with writing a scholarly treatise (*risāla 'ilmiyya*); he proceeds to spend no less than eight hours a day to attend to the

---

[20] See *Iqtiṣādunā*, 347.

questions directed to him from all over the world regarding issues related to acts of worship, transactions, the jurisprudence of relationships, the jurisprudence of the family, the jurisprudence of rights, the jurisprudence of medicine and health, the jurisprudence of the law, and the investment and distribution of wealth. These issues also include general and specific matters and varied intellectual concepts, and the position of religion toward all of them should be specified, precisely, soundly, and honestly. Throughout these hours while he makes this great effort, the *marjaʿ* is in the service of the Islamic *umma* and the knowledge of the family of Muḥammad ﷺ. This is what we mean when we say that jurisprudence is not simply a book about the rulings of purity, impurity, menstruation, and postnatal bleeding (*nifās*); jurisprudence is a system of life.

We already presented actual examples and proofs from the words of Sayyid al-Khūʾī ﵀ and his students about the comprehensiveness of the *Marjiʿiyyah* beyond the sphere of the lawful and the unlawful, and we will refer to this again when discussing Sayyid al-Sīstānī's scholarly personality.

The Importance of the Marjiʿiyyah

Martyr al-Ṣadr ﵀ proposed the idea of developing the *Marjiʿiyyah* from an individual level to an institutional level. According to this idea, the *Marjiʿiyyah* would be an institution managing the affairs of the Muslims all over the world, and it would have different apparatuses. One apparatus would be responsible for the issues of the *khums*, another for the legal issues of the Shīʿa, a third for doctrinal concepts, and a fourth that includes the most learned *marjaʿ* who supervises the religious aspects of the institution as a whole. This project that martyr al-Ṣadr ﷺ proposed was the subject of consideration and discussion among certain jurists. However, the circumstances have not allowed implementing it so far. We're actually speaking of the position of *Marjiʿiyyah* in its current reality here. The importance of this position becomes clear from the significant responsibilities and the great duties that the jurist has. These are several.

The first duty is teaching seminary students, educating the virtuous, and producing jurists and *mujtahids*. The political, social, and cultural Islamic arena cannot exist without a religious scholar. This scholar would have been educated by the jurist who is employed in the seminary, which means that the grace, thought, and all the positions and culture that we have go back to that jurist in the seminary. This is why al-Riḍā ﷺ said, "On the Day of Judgment, the worshipful man will be told, 'You were a praiseworthy man. You were concerned with yourself and spared people the trouble of worrying because of you, so enter into Paradise. The jurist is someone who bestows his goodness on other people, saves them from their enemies, provides them with the blessings of God's Paradises, and helps them attain

God's pleasure. The jurist will be told, 'O sponsor of the orphans of the family of Muḥammad and guide of the weak among their lovers and supporters, stand up and intercede for people who received knowledge or learned from you.' At this, he stands up and enters Paradise, with groups upon groups upon groups entering with him [Imām al-Riḍā repeated the word groups ten times]. These people are the ones who learned from him and who learned from others who learned from him, and who learned from those who learned from his students until the Day of Judgment. Notice how much God differentiated between the two positions [of the worshipful man and the jurist]."

The second duty of the jurist in the seminary is that he enlists the help of his virtuous students to always be aware of the misconceptions about Islam and Shīʿism and the recent innovations of intellectually wayward people. He either responds to these issues himself or assigns the job to his students, uncovering the falsity of these claims, putting a stop to innovations, and stopping the tribulations that occur in every age. This is because the Prophet ﷺ said, "If innovations emerge in my *umma*, let the scholar display his knowledge lest the curse of God be upon him."

This important role that the jurists have is highlighted in a narration by Imām al-Ṣādiq عليه السلام: "The scholars among our Shīʿa are stationed at the frontier of Īblīs and his demons (*ʿafārīt*), preventing them from attacking our weak Shī‘a and protecting these Shī‘a from coming under the authority of Īblīs and his Shī‘a, who are the enemies of the Ahl al-Bayt (*al-nawāṣib*). Whoever of our Shī‘a assumes this role is a thousand thousand times better than those who wage *jihād* against the Byzantines, the Turks, and the Khazar. This is because this person is protecting the religion of those who love us, which spares their bodies from harm."

The third duty of the jurist is developing precise theories in jurisprudence, the principles of jurisprudence, the science of transmitters, exegesis, and other sciences every day. Through this, the jurist contributes to the progress of Imāmī thought and ensures that it keeps up with the developments of civilization and its different intellectual domains. He also displays the greatness of the religion and the sect through the depth of his thought and the soundness of his words at all levels. The idea that comes from the jurist's pen is not less important than the sacrifices, efforts, and martyrs of the *umma* regarding the service that it contributes to Islam and its elevation. Al-Ṣādiq ﷺ even said, "On the Day of Judgment, God will gather all the people on one plane. The balances will be set up. Ihe blood of the martyrs will be weighed against the ink of the scholars, and the ink of the scholars will outweigh the blood of the martyrs."

For example, Sayyid al-Khū'ī's ﵀ works in jurisprudence, the principles of jurisprudence, the science of transmitters, and exegesis numbers up to eighty volumes. There is hardly a contemporary *marjaʿ*, jurist, virtuous person, student, or academic who can approach any topic or formulate any concept—whether in jurisprudence, its principles, or the science of transmitters—without going back to the works of Sayyid al-Khūʾī ﷻ and referring to them. No scholar is able to avoid this point of entry, i.e. Sayyid al-Khūʾī's ﷻ lectures, in any of the seminary's sciences. These lectures have been the primary aid of every researcher and intellectual. What service to Imāmī thought equals the service of this great figure and his students?

One of his most prominent students is the genius Sayyid Muḥammad al-Rūḥānī ﷻ, the author of *al-Muntaqā fil-Uṣūl* and *al-Murtaqā fil-Fiqh*, which contain many original ideas. Another student of his is the great intellectual Sayyid martyr Muḥammad Bāqir al-Ṣadr ﷻ who contributed to the development of the humanities in the fields of economics, logic, and philosophy. It is enough pride and honor for Sayyid al-Khūʾī ﷻ that the whole sect is indebted to him. Most jurists, *marājiʿ*, virtuous persons, researchers, and decision-makers in the Shīʿī world in the fields of politics and sociology are either his students or students of his students. He is the first source and the most trustworthy reference.

Among the most important achievements and roles of our famous *marājiʿ* are their eternal leadership roles.

Never once has the general *marājiʿiyya* of the Shīʿa been assumed by a dormant, reclusive, or oblivious scholar. The 1920 Iraqi Revolt stood on the shoulders of the *marājiʿ* of Shīʿism, such as Shaykh Muḥammad Taqī al-Shīrāzī ؒ and Shaykh al-Iṣfahānī ؒ. Imām al-Ḥakīm ؒ, in his leadership position, performed the greatest role, by fighting atheistic schools and unjust political parties. Imām Khomeini ؒ also undertook a great, unprecedented project, i.e. the Islamic Revolution in Iran, elevating the position of Islam all over the world.

Imām al-Khūʾī ؒ, the Sayyid of the sect, walked in the footsteps of his predecessors by constant giving through his institutions in the West, India, Pakistan, Thailand, as well as through his philanthropic projects in these and other countries. With his strength and iron will, he persisted on the path of steadfastness and patience under the clutches of the greatest tyrant of his time for twenty-five years. His associates were killed, his sons were assaulted, and he was put under very close watch.

Despite all these attempts, the monstrous regime of that time could elicit from Sayyid al-Khūʾī ؒ neither one word of support and blessing of itself nor one word of criticism against the Islamic Revolution in Iran. Throughout the eight years of relentless war, Sayyid al-Khūʾī ؒ preserved the seminary without giving in, growing weak, or changing his position toward the Baathist regime. He was patient, firm, and unwavering, cultivating the tree of religiosity in Iraq until he went to his Lord, an oppressed martyr. His great student Muḥammad Bāqir al-Ṣadr ﵀ was also like this, sacrificing himself for the sake of his principles and values. Martyr al-Ṣadr ﵀ was a symbol of *jihād* and sacrifice, and on his path of patience, *jihād*, and confrontation walked the great jurist Sayyid al-Sabziwārī ﵀. As for the positions of the great *marjaʿ* Sayyid al-Sīstānī and his character, I spoke about him extensively in holy Qum several years ago, and one of our dear brothers wrote this talk down and arranged it in the best way possible.

The reader might be wondering why I did not mention the other *marājiʿ* in Iraq and Iran although they have a well-known history at the scholarly and practical levels. The answer is that I limited myself in this short introduction to my own teachers as a sign of loyalty to them, especially that the achievements of some of them are not known; I only wanted to highlight these achievements. Otherwise, all the teachers of the seminary and the elect and chosen *marājiʿ* in Iran and Iraq have a primary, active role in preserving the religion and defending the sect.

To conclude, we ask God ﷻ to preserve all of our well-known *marājiʿ* who are the poles of the religion, to defend the sect and the religion through them, to protect them, and to protect this position from the schemes and dangerous plans of the enemies of the religion. We ask God to make the *umma* see the greatness of the position of the scholars and *marājiʿ*, and connect its members to these figures in all of their affairs. He is the guardian of success.

Homage to His Eminence,

Grand Āyatullāh Sayyid ʿAlī al-Ḥusaynī al-Sīstānī

بسم الله الرحمن الرحيم

In the Name of God, the Beneficent, the Merciful

In the name of God, and peace and blessings be upon Muḥammad, the noblest Prophet and Envoy, and upon his blessed pure family. My detailed talk about Sayyid al-Sīstānī is not out of disregard for our other great *marājiʿ*. I deeply honor and respect them all, especially my own teachers among them, such as the Grand Āyatullāh and jurist al-Muḥaqqiq Shaykh al-Waḥīd al-Khurāsānī, may God preserve him. Among them are also figures who are count as my teachers because I benefited from their research and vast works, such as Grand Āyatullāh and jurist Sayyid Muḥammad Ṣādiq al-Rūḥānī and Grand Āyatullāh and jurist Sayyid Muḥammad Saʿīd al-Ḥakīm قدس سره, in addition to other brilliant *marājiʿ* who are the pillars of the sect and the poles of Shīʿism.

My current talk aims to respond to some misconceptions and assaults that have been directed at the *Marjiʿiyyah* of Sayyid al-Sīstānī by the enemies of the truthful sect five years ago. Discussing the character of our teacher and refuge, the leader of the sect and the great *marjaʿ*, Sayyid al-Sīstānī is divided into three headlines: the features of his inborn character, the features of his acquired character, and the features of his scholarly character.

The Features of His Inborn Character

These are his natural attributes that he was known for from childhood; they are factors that have influenced the make-up of his great character at the level of leadership, knowledge, and mysticism. They are many.

The First Feature: He is an Avid Reader

Since his childhood, Sayyid al-Sīstānī was known for his intense desire to be alone with his books most of the time. He never cared about recreational trips or social relations. His friends were few, and he rarely participated in gatherings. He seldom joked, and his concern was to engage in scholarly or analytical discussions to the exclusion of all else. This was an important factor in the make-up of his cultural character such that he became like an encyclopedia of diverse branches of knowledge and various cultures, and his blessed person became an embodiment of a library.

The Second Feature: His Habit Is Harmony

From his childhood, Sayyid al-Sīstānī deeply disliked violence and division. He preferred calm and harmony, and he was a peaceful child who hated quarrels and confrontations even if he himself was being assaulted. His journey in holy Najaf, which was full of intellectual, political, and social conflicts, was spent without supporting one side over another, joining a movement, or supporting a political party or trend. He steered clear of all sources of tension, friction, and difference, and he did not waste his time on personal or social conflicts with others. This was to the extent that when the discussion became heated between him and his students during lessons, he preferred to remain quiet, not because he could not answer, but out of a desire to relieve the tension and resolve the disagreement.

This feature made his past a pure white page and earned him the love of all sides. It is also an important factor in what is known about his noble *Marjiʿiyyah*, as he became a compassionate father to all differing sides, bringing them together and unifying their word.

The Third Feature: His Attachment to Heaven

Sayyid al-Sīstānī grew up in holy Mashhad, in a home known for its worship and mysticism, so he became consumed with invocations (*adhkār*) and litanies (*awrād*). From his youth, he preferred solitude (*khulwa*), and he continued in this habit until he became a teacher in the seminary. Because of this, some of his contemporaries said that he was like a dervish or a monk. This spiritual inclination became a factor that influenced the makeup of his mystical character that is known for godliness (*waraʿ*), a deep fear of God ﷻ, and a distaste for empty temptations. His presence was and still is one that reminds those sitting with him of the Hereafter.

The Fourth Feature: Independence

Sayyid al-Sīstānī has an independent character in two regards. First, he hates the spirit of dependency and relying on other people. He always did his errands himself and depended on his intellect and his own decisions from his youth. This gave rise to his unique ambition. He went to the seminaries of Mashhad, Qum, and Najaf, and met with all sorts of different teachers in search of those most capable of satisfying his scholarly appetite and his academic ambitions. During his days of study in Najaf, he was known to be one of the students who most visited the different libraries, relying on himself to reach the trusted sources or seeking out the soundest opinion that leads to acceptance and conviction.

Second, his tendency to be independent caused him not to be tied to a certain side and not to walk in the shadow of another, regardless of whether they are parties or individuals. This contributed to his leadership and the formation of his stances and decisions. He has never come under the influence of his entourage, children, or relatives. He's always been independent in his decisions and stances, which he reaches after consultation, contemplation, and deep study.

The Features of His Acquired Character

These are the attributes that Sayyid al-Sīstānī acquired due to his life experiences and his engagement in a domain filled with difficulties and political and social changes.

The First Feature: Insight and Far-Sightedness

Leadership does not result from a position or an election, nor is it inherited. Leadership is a stance. Wise leadership depends on making an influential decision during the right time and in an effective way, which requires far-sightedness and the ability to read the present reality and anticipate the future, examining it slowly and deliberately. This applies to the character of our Sayyid and teacher [Sayyid al-Sīstānī]. This is verified by his decisions, his stances during the events of Najaf and Samarra, and his stance from the parliamentary and local elections. Those who disagree with him may describe him as slow in making decisions. However, he believes that the disadvantages of rushing and making immature decisions outweigh the disadvantages of delaying and taking one's time. In dealing with different events, Sayyid al-Sīstānī always had the habit of considering the possible consequences on the *umma* as a whole, including its elites, when making any influential decision.

This was his habit in the past as well. Sayyid al-Sīstānī was the one who suggested to his teacher Sayyid al-Khū'ī ☙, during the 1991 uprising, the formation of a committee tasked with considering the internal and external sources of the uprising's longevity before making any political or administrative decisions about it. This was because Sayyid al-Sīstānī was anticipating the future due to his knowledge of the brutal regime that was in power at the time.

The Second Feature: Being Realistic

Many leaders may take advantage of political or social circumstances to gain new titles or develop a reputation. Such people make sure to participate in any new trend to polish their image or expand their social influence. However, a leader who is loyal to his *ummah* makes sure to be realistic in dealing with the different circumstances. He gives priority to the most important matters over less important matters and uses bad things to offset worse things (*daf' al-afsad bil-fāsid*) in context of the general interests of Islamic society.

This applies to the stances of Sayyid al-Sīstānī. He could have taken advantage of the American occupation of Iraq to issue legal decrees calling for *jihād* and armed resistance in order to gain a reputation throughout the Islamic and Arab *umma* and become a hero of Arab identity. However, he dealt with the event realistically, focusing on the public interests of the Iraqi people as far as possible. He did not decree that it was obligatory to engage in armed resistance against the occupation, but he didn't prohibit this either. This is for two reasons.

First, Sayyid al-Sīstānī knew that the Iraqi people, who were wronged for thirty-five years, paid the price with their blood, and tens of thousands of them were wounded. Their tragedies and the casualties among them are countless. Out of loyalty to them and due to a desire to preserve their blood, honor, and money, a leader who loves his people does not make it obligatory for them to shed more blood and offer many casualties. This is particularly because a large segment of the Iraqi people was already fed up with wounds and tragedies; these people preferred to find rest and tend to their injuries.

Second, dealing with things realistically regardless of emotions and reactions requires considering things within the framework of the important and the more important. Sayyid al-Sīstānī considered that driving the occupation out of Iraq was important, but that it was more important to give the Iraqi people a chance to build a political system of their own choice that is selected and elected by them.

If someone had issued a legal decree that made it obligatory to drive the occupation out, and the Iraqi people made thousands of sacrifices in blood and lives for three years or more, they wouldn't have earned the reward of the battle themselves. Saddam's Baathist regime and al-Qaeda both were at the height of their military and intelligence power at the time all over the country. This made either of them a leadership that was prepared to take advantage of the situation and seize the opportunity to control the country again as soon as the occupation was out. In that case, they would've ruled with an iron fist and spread corruption on the earth like they did in the past. The experience of the Algerian people and other people who sacrificed thousands of lives in revolutions and movements ended with a small segment of society earning the reward. It was this segment that controlled society and assumed its leadership.

For this reason, the most important and best thing for the sake of public interest was for the Iraqi people to devote themselves to establishing a political and social leadership of their own choice and conviction, healing their wounds, and building their cultural, charitable, and scholarly institutions. Once the Iraqi people had a strong, proud existence, they would be able to drive out the occupation using different and various methods.

Giving priority to the most important matters over less important matters is bitter, difficult, and contradictory to heated feelings and emotions. However, such a step is in harmony with the wisdom, realistic outlook, and loyalty of [Sayyid al-Sīstānī's] leadership.

In addition, Sayyid al-Sīstānī did not prohibit armed leadership, nor did he ever accept into his presence any side that collaborated with or represented the occupation. He only referred to the American and British presence in Iraq as an occupation, and he continues to do so until this day. He insisted on holding the elections, although the Americans' scheme was to install a government loyal to them using certain methods. Sayyid al-Sīstānī also insisted on not making any strategic agreements with the American side unless they contained two elements: 1- preserving the sovereignty and independence of Iraq and 2- conducting a national consensus about accepting and engaging with the agreement.

Our dear brother and researcher Ḥāmid al-Khaffāf collected from Sayyid al-Sīstānī's book *al-Riḥla al-'Ilājiyya* his statements that aimed to resolve the situation and defend the sanctity of the religion and the dignity of the Iraqi people. They numbered ninety-six key statements in total that constitute important raw material about Iraq's contemporary history.

The Third Feature: A Fatherly Spirit

Wise leadership elevates itself from divisive conflicts and social differences, being a reference to its people regardless of their affiliations and opinions. This is embodied in Sayyid al-Sīstānī's wise leadership. He is a person who lived for fifty years or more in Iraq, and he witnessed many intellectual, political, and social differences. With his penetrating vision, he realized that these differences caused a serious fracture in the body of the *umma* and were an important factor in depleting its power and wasting its efforts. The *umma* became occupied with these differences and disregarded essential and crucial issues although the common points among the members of the *umma* are up to 80%. In contrast, the differences within the *umma* are no more than 10%. Sayyid al-Sīstānī has believed that the common thread between the differing sides, which unites them together, is coming together under the shadow of Muḥammad's family.

For this reason, Sayyid al-Sīstānī made sure to shower everyone with his fatherly tenderness, humility, and care, containing those who opposed him and differed with him using kind words and sincere advice. One of the features of his fatherly attitude is the way he deals with political leaders in Iraq. Sometimes he is tough on them, and sometimes he's kind. If he considers that it is best to invite them to visit him, advise them, and guide them, he will do so. However, if he considers that they need to be reprimanded and disciplined at times due to slacking in their duty of securing the people's best interests, he will not allow them to visit him.

The Fourth Feature: Being One with the Greatness of Islam and Faith

Conscious leadership does not get distracted by secondary, marginal causes at the expense of major and primary causes. Sayyid al-Sīstānī displayed this in his actions, movement, and habits. He considers that the most important cause for a *marjaʿ* of the *umma* and a Muslim leader is defending the sanctity of Islam and the Imāmī sect, keeping their image pure and their reputation spotless in the sight of rational society in general. Sayyid al-Sīstānī believes that the sanctity of Islam and the faith is stronger than the sanctity of the believer and any other sanctity. For this reason, he issued a legal decree that a Muslim cannot seize the money of a non-Muslim in Islamic and non-Islamic countries except in legal and rational ways. This is because of the pledge of security that exists among the members of different nations. Sayyid al-Sīstānī's aim was to preserve the reputation of Islam and its leadership, becoming a safe haven for the oppressed Iraqi people.

In several of his statements, he prohibited shedding the blood of other denominations of Iraqi, Arab, and Islamic society as a whole. This includes Christians, Jews, Sabians, and Yezidis who have not dedicated themselves to combatting Islam or violating the sanctities of the Muslims. Sayyid al-Sīstānī also made it unlawful to seize their money and called for giving them their full social and national rights at the same level with the Muslims. This was to give a pure image of Islam as a religion rich with humanitarian principles that respects all of humanity and to say that Islamic leadership showers its fatherly tenderness on non-Muslim constituents as well so that all may benefit from Islam's leniency, kindness, and care.

One of Sayyid al-Sīstānī's most important stances, which shows his concern for the sanctity of Islam and its greatness, was displayed when he strictly faced the sectarian strife that aimed to disrupt the unified Iraqi society. He emphasized that it is prohibited for any Iraqi to shed the blood of the members of other Muslim sects, stressing that they are all brothers in Islam and have the rights of brotherhood. Sayyid al-Sīstānī did not do this out of weakness or flattery, nor was he seeking a reputation or titles. He only did it because the sanctity of Islam, including its propagation and power and displaying its leniency and parental comprehensiveness, is a primary cause that cannot be disregarded. His stances concerning the incidents of Samarra and his statements in support of the persecuted Palestinian people are among the clearest proofs of his deep concern for the sanctity and greatness of Islam.

The Fifth Feature: "O World, Find Someone Else to Tempt"

Some people who reach leadership positions may try to abuse their positions by amassing fortunes for them and their children or using their positions as an opportunity to pass down properties, real estate, and money in their wills. The *Marji'iyyah* of Sayyid al-Sīstānī is in complete opposition to that. Since the days of his youth, he practiced the words of his grandfather the Commander of the Believers ﷺ: "Every person who is led has a leader [Imām] whom he follows and whose knowledge he uses as a source of light. Your own Imām sufficed himself of his world with two worn garments and of his meals with two loaves." For dozens of years, Sayyid al-Sīstānī has been living in a hut of Najaf's old huts, paying rent on time each month and living the life of one who renounces worldly appearances without caring about pleasures or temptations. His clothes, furniture, and meals after his *Marji'iyyah* are the same as when he was thirty years old and living on a small stipend received from some of his teachers.

He made it forbidden to himself and to his children to own a house, a car, or any expensive device, and he made it forbidden to himself and to his children to accept any gift that could create an unconscious preference for the gift-giver over others. He did not agree to the suggestion of being personally provided with electricity by the Iraqi government or receiving a kind of residency that is not available to the members of his people, quoting the words of Imām ʿAlī ﷺ: "God obliged the Imāms of justice to equate themselves with the weakest of the people so that a poor person's poverty does not become too much to bear."

The environment in which he lived in holy Qum as a child was an environment of asceticism and renunciation of the world's frills and appearances. This made him hate to occupy himself with anything that implies vanity and worldliness. Sayyid al-Sīstānī has refused making appearances in different media outlets except in cases of extreme necessity in order to preserve his noble soul through piety and the godliness of avoiding any worldly or material pleasures.

He also forbade his agents and the people who emulate him anywhere in the world from displaying pictures of him or highlighting him to the exclusion of other *marājiʿ*. He also forbade them from establishing satellite channels or websites that speak about him or praise his *Marjiʿiyyah* or leadership. This is because he did not want the Imāmī leadership of Imām ʿAlī ﷺ to be branded as obsessed with publicity and the flattery of the media. If you see him and sit with him, you will know that the words of Imām ʿAlī ﷺ: "O world, find someone else to tempt" are his motto in public and in private.

Some loyal adherents may think that the way that the *Marjiʿiyyah* addresses the people and the *umma* through statements that come out of the *marjaʿ's* house implies a kind of contempt and belittlement of the *umma*. Such people believe that starting a television channel for the *Marjiʿiyyah* that presents the leader and *marjaʿ* when he speaks to his children in videos in his own voice, broadcasts the *Marjiʿiyyah's* daily news, and displays its statements and visions during all circumstances would be a civilized display of fatherliness and transparency. This channel, they say, would be a key factor in deepening the connection between the leader and his *umma*.

However, Sayyid al-Sīstānī has a different view that includes several factors. Respecting the *umma* and being loyal to it are not about establishing television channels, engaging in media mobilization, and occupying the people with the leader's photos, statements, and words. Respect and loyalty are about practical achievements on the ground. This is why Sayyid al-Sīstānī believes that establishing respect for the *umma*, being loyal to it, and consoling it does not take place through the media. It happens through his certified agents when they establish centers for doctrinal sciences, spend thousands to help the poor, build hospitals, and supply public development and civil institutions. Examples include Rafed Network for Cultural Development, Hodhod children's channel, the cities built to house students of the religious sciences in

Qum and Najaf, and other similar services. This is although Sayyid al-Sīstānī himself lives the life of the poor within his own home. For this reason, during many uprisings and movements, his mode of action was taking effective practical steps, not issuing fiery statements.

Second, if Sayyid al-Sīstānī undertook launching his own channel, it would be the start of the phenomenon of the *marājiʿ* having channels of their own. After that, you will find every *Marjiʿiyyah* supporting its own channel, which creates space for disagreement, heated competition, and the distraction of the *umma* with secondary matters at the expense of primary matters.

Third, choosing the proper circumstances for making appearances and getting the *umma* used to the fact that the *Marjiʿiyyah* only speaks about complex and important issues makes its statements more effective and motivating than a multiplicity of statements and overused propositions. To repeat, Sayyid al-Sīstānī's ingrained characteristic of disliking showing off and fleeting worldly things is actually an important reason for his abstaining from media appearances.

The Sixth Feature: True Certitude

You may have seen many people who make a show of their eager worship and belonging to the mystics and those attached to the world of dominion (*ʿālam malakūt*). Our great Sayyid, however, embodies in his actions and behaviors the famous saying of the sacred mystic, Sayyid ʿAlī al-Qāḍī 🕮: "Those who arrive do not speak about it, and those who speak about it never arrive." Sayyid al-Sīstānī spends a lot of time by himself, on the roof of his house, looking at the dome of his grandfather, the Commander of the Believers 🕮, remembering his way and contemplating his life and methodology. The words said in praise of his grandfather 🕮 apply to Sayyid al-Sīstānī himself: "He held himself accountable in private and wrung his hands about past events." Sayyid al-Sīstānī takes special delight in the remembrance of God and voluntary prayers, but he never publicized his belonging to the world of the mystics or boasted about being of the people of worship and remembrance of God. When he was still able to leave his house, he habitually visited the tomb of his grandfather, the Commander of the Faithful 🕮, particularly the Great Mosque of Kufa, as well as al-Sahla Mosque, at times when only a few people may be able to see him.

In addition, even some of his closest associates do not know about his relationships with the sincere mystics of Najaf. The most important thing for him is the true certitude that exists between him and his Lord, not the impression of other people. However, if you sit with him, you will find that a great indication of his worshipful nature and mystical spirit is that he is a manifestation of the *ḥadīth* from al-Ṣādiq 🕮. When al-

Ṣādiq ﷺ was asked about the Prophet's ﷺ saying, "Looking at the faces of the scholars is worship," the Imām ﷺ said, "A scholar is the one who reminds you of the Hereafter when you look at him."

The Features of His Scholarly Character

Undoubtedly, the position of *Marji'iyyah* implies the knowledge of all the sciences related to legal derivation and determining the religious ruling. These sciences include language, exegesis, and theology. The jurist should be knowledgeable and perceptive about all of these sciences. All the famous *marāji'* who are teachers in the seminary are like this; their skills are not limited to jurisprudence and its principles. This fact requires a detailed discussion of the scholarly character of the great man Sayyid al-Sīstānī. We will speak of the scholarly methodology of Sayyid al-Sīstānī's lectures on three fields within the seminary: the principles of jurisprudence, jurisprudence, and the science of transmitters.

The Principles of Jurisprudence

Sayyid al-Sīstānī has a unique methodology in the principles of jurisprudence that differs from the course of many masters and teachers of this science. This may be made clear by presenting the features of his school in the principles of jurisprudence.

A Comprehensive Vision

Before Sayyid al-Sīstānī discusses any matter within the principles of jurisprudence and goes into its details, he takes a comprehensive view of it in order to determine its general components that influence its acceptance or rejection. In doing this, he separates these general components from the secondary and partial components, which gives every researcher discussing the matter a special insight. This differs from the methodology of many teachers who discuss matters in a piece-meal way, going from one section to the next in a way that mixes up general and particular components.

Vast Cultural Knowledge

Just like Sayyid al-Sīstānī is skilled in jurisprudence, the principles of jurisprudence, the science of transmitters, philosophy, and exegesis, he also has vast cultural knowledge. He is an avid reader of certain branches of the humanities such as psychology, sociology, and law, particularly Egyptian, Iraqi, and French law. In addition, he is greatly informed about history, and especially the political history of Arab and Islamic states. This cultural knowledge even had an effect on his discussions of the principles of jurisprudence. He benefited from linguistics in differentiating between the kinds of indication (*al-dalāla*) in the chapter on concepts, differentiating between the forms of government, and discussing the variety within the language of revelation in the texts as presented in his discussion on the rule of no harm (*lā ḍarar*).

He also benefited from the mathematical proof of probability in analyzing the authority of consensus (*ijmā'*) and recurrent reports (*al-khabar al-mutawātir*). In addition, he benefited from law in proposing the theory of implicitness (*istibṭān*) to explain the reality of declaratory rulings (*al-ḥukm al-waḍ'ī*) and their relation to defining rulings (*al-ḥukm al-taklīfī*). Sayyid al-Sīstānī also used psychology to analyze the rational motivation of religious obligations by considering the soul based on probability, the importance of the probable consequence, and the effects of the deed. His eager spirit, which rejuvenates itself, shines, and presides over his creative thought, still yearns to know about all new things although he passed his eightieth year. No sooner than a book reaches him on any topic that he eagerly sets out to read it.

A Spirit of Rejuvenation

Sayyid al-Sīstānī's discussions are neither a repetition of others' words nor an imitation of what has been said in the commentaries and glosses of *Kifāyat al-Uṣūl*. He always distinguishes himself in his discussions, either in formulating his propositions, adding certain details to them, or choosing an unprecedented methodology. A quick glance at his works on the principles of jurisprudence reveals many methodologies and details unique to him, either because he created them himself or because he expanded them and presented them in a new way.

One example is the theory of conceptual sameness (*huwahuwiyya taṣawwuriyya*) that he used in explaining the declarative relation (*ʿalaqa waḍʿiyya*) between utterance and meaning. Another example is when he used the theory of the supplement of applied making (*mutammim al-jaʿl al-taṭbīqī*) when discussing religious reality (*al-ḥaqīqa al-sharʿiyya*). A third example is his discussion of the degrees of actual expression of the derivative based on the diversity of apparent and hidden principles, and his analysis of the derivative's simplicity at the level of the primary intelligible (*al-maʿqūl al-awwalī*) that does not contradict its make-up according to the secondary intelligible (*al-maʿqūl al-thānawī*).

Another thing that Sayyid al-Sīstānī is famous for is his analysis of the truth of defining rulings and authoritative commands (*al-amr mawlawī*) based on two elements: the element of resurrection and the punitive element (reward or punishment). He is also known for his theory of amalgamated necessity (*al-wujūb al-indimājī*) in his premise on the necessary (*al-wājib*), and his assertion of the different degrees of ability (*qudra*) in their relation to defining rulings. In this regard, he said that ability itself influences the phase of actuality, and complete ability influences the phase of agency (*fāʿiliyya*) and the effectuation of liability (*tanajjuz*).

Sayyid al-Sīstānī also said that it is not logical to have a gradational relationship between two equal and conflicting things (*al-mutazāḥimayn al-mutasāwiyayn*), and that the theme of obligation in such a case is the common abstract category (*al-jāmiʿ al-intizāʿī*), referred to as the one (*al-aḥad*). Sayyid al-Sīstānī benefited from the theory of Aqā ʿAlī Mudarris ﷺ, which states that the accident is not an existent beyond the existence of the essence but a kind of essential existence. This theory comes as part of the distinction between annexational and unificational composition under the discussion of the combination of commands and prohibitions.

In his discussion of the absolute and the limited, Sayyid al-Sīstānī discussed the difference between absoluteness in teaching and absoluteness in issuing legal decrees, and listed their different effects. Of these effects is that the certain limit at the level of rhetoric adversely affects absoluteness at the level of issuing legal decrees but not at the level of teaching. In addition, combining the limited and the absolute, in all their forms, is a customary combination of rhetoric at the level of teaching. However, if the absoluteness at the level of issuing legal decrees is based on dispensation (*tarkhīṣ*), and the separate restrictive element is mandatory after the time of performing the deed was past, the two can be combined by restrictiveness, as is stated in the principles of jurisprudence, as a delay in explaining the rhetoric from the time of its being needed, which is disliked by custom.

Of Sayyid al-Sīstānī's theories is his discussion of the authoritativeness of certainty, stating that this authoritativeness, or its status of being an excuse before God, is not intrinsic but rational. This is because it concerns certainty that comes from a rational source. Sayyid al-Sīstānī also discussed the issue of committing an act with the mistaken belief that it is a sin (*al-tajarrī*),[21] stating that motivation and deserving punishment upon disobedience is based on theoretical reason's knowledge of the implicit authoritative command contained in the punishment. It is not based on practical reason's judgment of obedience and the repugnance (*qubḥ*) of rebelling against the Master and taking Him lightly.

---

21 [Translator's note]: For more on the concept, see the following: "But what happens if an agent acts in defiance of a justified belief that turns out to be false? John may for example actually drink water, falsely believing it to be white wine, and thus accepting that he is disregarding a divine command (not realizing, of course, that he is not in reality). This sort of action is called *tajarrī* and the agent in question is called *mutajarrī*." Amir Mohammad Emami and Mirza Mohammad Kazem Askari, "Tajarrī as Religious Luck," in *Philosophy and Jurisprudence in the Islamic World* 1/198.

Regarding liability in the case of general knowledge of the ruling, Sayyid al-Sīstānī says that its categorical liability is intellectual, whereas its liability in reality is rational. Concerning the matter of rational license (*al-barā'a al-'aqliyya*), Sayyid al-Sīstānī says that it does not concern any kind of doubt about the obligation, but doubt that is not probable based on determining the level of probability. He also says that the continuance applies to classificatory confusion (*shubha ḥukmiyya*) based on non-contradiction. He also says that the continuance of the limitedness of making is a proven principle, not that it affects the thing that is made positively or negatively, which is the opinion of al-Muḥaqqiq al-Nā'īnī 🕮.

Sayyid al-Sīstānī also created a new avenue in the discussion of contradiction, which is his chapter on the origin of differences in *ḥadīths*, and which effectively addresses the issue of contradiction within the texts. In the domain of analyzing the narrations that include solutions for contradictory evidence, Sayyid al-Sīstānī says that contradictory evidence does not imply devotional preponderance (*tarjīḥ*) but guidance. This is because there is a difference between the authoritative and the non-authoritative. Preponderance in this regard goes back, in Sayyid al-Sīstānī's opinion, to a rational principle based on doubting each difference categorically.

These are only a few examples of the many details that Sayyid al-Sīstānī contributed to the principles of jurisprudence.

Combining Legal Schools

Sayyid al-Sīstānī's methodology is based on combining the six jurisprudential school: the school of al-Shaykh al-Aʿẓam [Shaykh al-Anṣārī قدس سره], the school of the author of *al-Kifāya* (Mullā Muḥammad Kāẓim al-Khurāsānī قدس سره), the school of al-Muḥaqqiq al-Ṭihrānī قدس سره, the school of al-Muḥaqqiq al-Nāʾīnī قدس سره, the school of al-ʿIrāqī قدس سره, and the school of al-Iṣfahānī قدس سره. Sayyid al-Sīstānī then judges these schools in terms of the essential additions they made to a certain issue.

A Rational View

One of the most important features of Sayyid al-Sīstānī's jurisprudential work is discussing and then separating the philosophical themes that are based on abstract rational proofs from the jurisprudential issue that is under discussion. He also insists on tying this jurisprudential issue to rational, legal principles. He used this approach in discussing the conditional necessary, gradation, and other topics.

The Field of Jurisprudence

The research of Sayyid al-Sīstānī in the field of jurisprudence is distinguished by seven features that satisfy the knowledge-seeker because they encompass matters in detail and lead to reaching the soundest and most precise opinions. These features are:

The First Feature: Historical Background

Sayyid al-Sīstānī begins his presentation of the matter as it was presented for the first time in the first jurisprudential book that has reached us, regardless of whether it is of the books of the Shīʿīs or the Sunnīs. It is undoubtable that tracing the path and expansion of the issue is related to authenticating statements about it and knowing the extent of its relation to the heart of the matter.

The Second Feature: The Books of the Ancients

Sayyid al-Sīstānī focuses on referring back to the books of the ancients and closely examines their wording because doing so is closely related to discovering what they considered basic lived principles. These lived principles did not reach us because the authors were the first ones to receive the texts, and they are closer to the texts' time, which makes those authors more capable of reading the texts' temporal and basic proofs. Doing so is also related to knowing the extent of the ruling and whether it belongs to the category of fame (*shuhra*), consensus (*imjāʿ*), unanimity (*tasālum*), or necessity.

The Third Feature: Context

One of the main features of Sayyid al-Sīstānī's methodology is reading Sunnī books of jurisprudence and *ḥadīth* about all issues because many narrations are simply a response to the Sunnī opinion, proving it incorrect or making additions to it. Reading the statements of the Sunnīs on a given issue reveals the contemporary atmosphere of the narration of the infallible ﷺ and constitutes proof of its content. An example is the opinion of a number of known scholars on the obligation of paying the *khums* tax on land bought from a non-Muslim (*dhimmī*).

The Fourth Feature: An Abundance of Proofs

Sayyid al-Sīstānī's methodology is that authority is achieved through certainty and not through a trustworthy report. For this reason, he makes sure to collect all the different proofs that inspire trustworthiness in a narration. Of these proofs is the well-known application of the narration (*shuhrat al-ʿamal bil-riwāya*) and its agreement with the general principles and foundations that are deduced from the Book and the noble *sunna*. Sayyid al-Sīstānī's methodology is based on the idea that the meaning of the preponderating factor (*al-murajjiḥ*), referred to in the narrations on preponderance as agreeing with the Book, is agreement with the spirit of the text. Some texts express this concept by the Imām's ﷺ saying, "Measure it against the Book of God and our reports." An example is the fame of the narration's content in the books of *ḥadīth*, language, and literature.

The Fifth Feature: Expertise in Ḥadīth Books

Sayyid al-Sīstānī's jurisprudential research involves great experience with manuscript copies of the four books as well as other *ḥadīth* books. He is precise in tracing and comparing differences among these copies, and is well-equipped to give preference to some copies over others. You cannot find this in a lot of other kinds of research that is done in the seminary.

There is a famous belief that *al-Kāfī* is more precise than *al-Tahdhībayn* [*al-Tahdhīb* and *al-Istibṣār*], which leads to preferring the sources of *al-Kāfī* over other sources. However, there is no proof of this, and Sayyid al-Sīstānī believes that there are actually proofs to the contrary.

The Sixth Feature: Deductive Apparentness

In the discussion on the authoritativeness of apparentness (*al-ẓuhūr*) within the principles of jurisprudence, Sayyid al-Sīstānī holds that the authoritative apparentness is customary apparentness and not self-evident apparentness. One of the examples of objective apparentness is particular apparentness. Each codifier has a particular way of expressing himself and particular terms that he uses. For this reason, it is incorrect, according to custom, to glean the actual purpose of any law by weighing it against general customary understanding because each codifier uses his own way of speaking to formulate laws.

Examples include the *ḥadīths* of Ahl al-Bayt 🕮. An expert in these *ḥadīths* knows that they employ particular wording and a unique style, and that there are common allusions (*ma'ārīḍ*) in the Imāms' 🕮 words. Many texts focused on this aspect, with some of them stating: "One of you will not be a jurist until he knows our style of speech. Our speech contains different aspects that are all correct." Other texts state: "Our words have an external and an internal aspect." This requires the jurist to have a lot of experience in the jurisprudence of the narrations in order to reach authoritativeness, which is deductive apparentness or the meaning that is gleaned from combining the different meanings.

The Seventh Feature: Linguistic Skill

Understanding many of the texts, especially the Qur'ān and the *sunna*, requires knowing the rules of the Arabic language. The meaning of the texts cannot be determined simply by referring to a dictionary, such as *al-Munjid* or *al-Rāʾid*. One should refer back to primary lexicons, such as *Ṣiḥāḥ al-Lugha*, *al-Qāmūs*, and *Lisān al-ʿArab*, and know the earlier and later books among them to know which are closer to the time of the text itself. This also requires knowledge of the books of language, such as *Mufradāt* al-Raghib, *Asās al-Balāgha*, *Fiqh al-Lugha*, and others, in addition to referring to literature books to become familiar with the texts of the Arabs who lived in the time of the Qurʾānic revelation, or the time of the Prophet ﷺ or Imām ʿAlī عليه السلام.

The Science of Transmitters

Experience

One of the characteristics of Sayyid al-Sīstānī is that he is a master of the science of transmitters. His skill and great knowledge are clear at different levels of this science. He has expertise in different Sunnī and Shīʿī books about the science of transmitters, and he knows the purpose behind each book, which is important because it affects the categories of trustworthiness and weakness in them.

Distinguishing Earlier and Later Books

Sayyid al-Sīstānī also distinguishes between earlier and later books about the science of transmitters in order to determine whether the criticism and praise (*al-jarḥ wal-ta'dīl*) are foundational or inherited.

Different Kinds of Trustworthiness

He also focuses on the different ways of implying trustworthiness such as praise, expressing pleasure about a certain transmitter (*taraḍḍī*), expressing explicit trustworthiness, describing a transmitter as relating sound *ḥadīths* or having good narration, or saying that a transmitter's *ḥadīth* cannot be rejected. The difference in expressions is not just a matter of taste; it has to do with the trustworthiness of the narrator and the reliability of the narration in proving a certain ruling that goes against the established principles. Each scholar of the science of transmitters has his own terms that he uses and that are only known by people who have experience in his books.

Collecting Proofs

Sayyid al-Sīstānī, may God extend his blessed life, believes that the judgment of the scholar of the science of transmitters is not a testimony but an intuitive opinion. The words of these scholars constitute one of the proofs of trustworthiness. This requires collecting different proofs from *ḥadīth* books, jurisprudence books, and literature books about the fame of a narrator, his possession of a certificate of transmission (*ijāza*), and his acceptance or rejection by the Sunnīs.

All this influences a narrator's trustworthiness in the Shīʿī view.

The Art of Preponderance

Giving preference to the opinion of al-Najāshī ﵀ over Shaykh al-Ṭūsī ﵀ and giving preference to the opinion of al-Kashshī ﵀ over them both comes from inductive experience in all three books. It also requires knowing the precision and skill contained in each book at the level of criticism and praise and the value of the sources used by the authors of these books.

The Narrator's Knowledge

One of the proofs of a narrator's trustworthiness lies in examining his different narrations because their contents are an indication of his knowledge. This helps to determine whether he usually narrates things that contradict the rules or go against the principles of theology or whether the substance of his narrations agrees with the general tenets of the primordial religion and the pure law.

The Narrator's Position

Determining the narrator's position and whether he is a *mujtahid* or a *ḥadīth* transmitter also influences the trustworthiness of the content he is narrating from the infallible ﵇.

I do not forget to mention that one of God's ﷻ gifts to Sayyid al-Sīstānī is that He gave him two sons who are honored jurists and who are of the notable teachers in the seminary of holy Najaf. Their scholarly work is of benefit to the people of virtue and precision.

Lastly, the features of Sayyid al-Sīstānī's character that we mentioned are a few indicators that display the greatness of the position of *Marjiʿiyyah*. The attention of the Creator ﷻ and Imām al-Mahdī عجّل الله تعالى فرجه الشريف to this important position influences the choice of a handful of people from tens of thousands of seminary students [to become *marājiʿ*]. This is due to these people's competence, capability, and good reputation from childhood, which makes them fit for this great position.

In conclusion of our presentation of a few bright allusions to our great Sayyid's character, we should point out that recognizing the greatness of our *marājiʿ* is a way of recognizing the greatness of our Imāms عليهم السلام and a door to God's ﷻ knowledge, blessing, and wisdom.

Praise be to God, the Lord of all worlds

Holy Qum

www.ingramcontent.com/pod-product-compliance
Lightning Source LLC
Chambersburg PA
CBHW030916140626
46545CB00017B/2380
* 9 7 8 1 9 5 6 2 7 6 1 8 3 *